Tai Chi
PENG

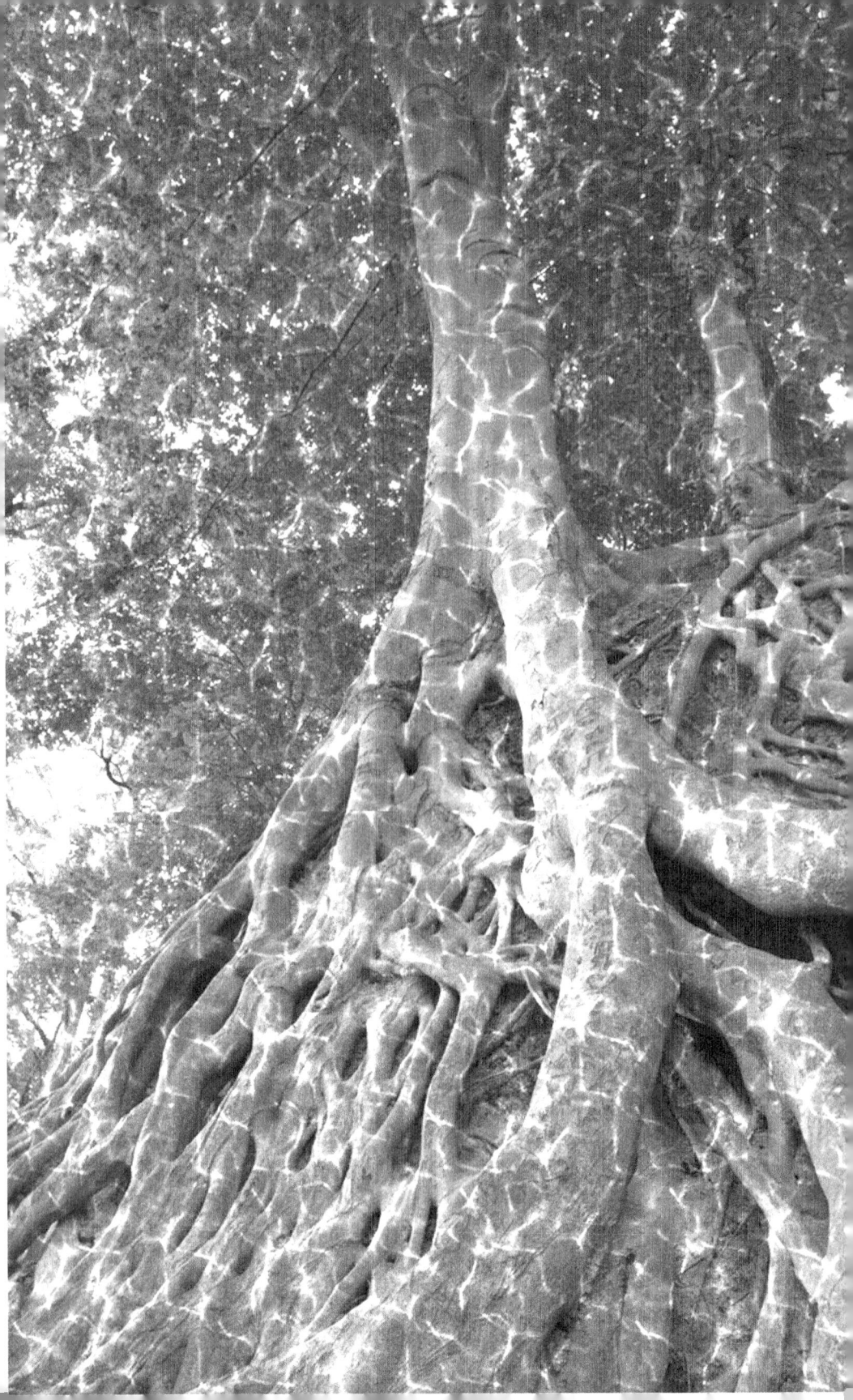

Tai Chi
PENG

Root Power Rising

by Scott Meredith

Illustrated by Jeremy Ray

Copyright © 2014 Scott Meredith

The moral right of the author has been asserted.

All rights reserved.

No part of this publication may be reproduced, stored in a retrieval system, or transmitted, in any form or by any means, without the prior permission in writing of the publisher, nor be otherwise circulated in any form of binding or cover other than that in which it is published and without a similar condition including this condition being imposed on the subsequent purchaser.

ISBN: 978-1-4953-1105-5

Typesetting services by BOOKOW.COM

Dedication

To the memory of the master jeweler,

WANG ZONGYUE

王宗岳

who cut, polished, and set Tai Chi –

the mysteriously radiant gem.

To the greatest Tai Chi master

of his generation,

BENJAMIN PANG JENG LO

羅邦楨

who is in no way responsible

for any part of this wild book.

Notes

All translations from the Chinese and Japanese are the original copyrighted work of the author unless otherwise explicitly sourced.

Most Chinese characters are traditional, with occasional variation including adoption of simplified characters, based on common usage, personal preference, and accepted historical precedent in names, among other criteria.

Most Chinese transliterations are Pinyin, with occasional variation including adoption of Wade-Giles and other variants, based on common usage, personal preference, and accepted historical precedent in names, among other criteria.

All drawings are original works produced for this book. Artwork concept and design by Scott Meredith and Jeremy Ray. Illustrations by Jeremy Ray. All pictures copyright © 2014 Scott Meredith. Anatomical diagrams are derived in part from licensed 3rd-party graphic materials, Copyright © 2014 Scott Meredith. Photograph of Mongolian wrestler and Sumo champion Byamba by Santiago Heredia, used with permission.

Disclaimer

All practices, processes, and methods described in this book are provided for entertainment purposes only. All martial arts practices including Tai Chi entail risks including, but not limited to, permanent disability and death.

Never engage in any physical practice except under the oversight of currently certified and licensed health care professionals.

Do not attempt anything described in this book without the full knowledge, consent, and personal supervision of a qualified, currently licensed physician or other qualified health care professional. This book may not be used to diagnose or treat any medical condition.

The publisher and author are not responsible for any specific health or allergy needs that may require medical supervision and are not liable for any damages or negative consequences from any treatment, action, application or preparation, to any person reading or following the information in this book.

The author and publisher make no representations or warranties of any kind and assume no liabilities of any kind with respect to the accuracy or completeness of the contents and specifically disclaim any implied warranties of merchantability or fitness of use for a particular purpose.

Neither the author nor the publisher shall be held liable or responsible to any person or entity with respect to any loss or incidental or consequential damages caused, or alleged to have been caused, directly or indirectly, by the information or programs contained herein.

Protect yourself at all times.

Contents

Introduction	1
Tai Chi and PENG Energy	4
Song of PENG	9
Energetic Architecture	16
Energy Hotspots	22
Practice Principles	33
The Circle-Slice Sword Drill	40
7 Poses: Structural Basics	48
Insubstantial and Substantial Leg	62
7 Poses: Relaxation Protocol	66
Feeling the Hard Wave	76
7 Poses: Zhangzhuang Overview	92
7 Poses: The Microreactivation Method	100
The Final Principle: Waist Activation & Cloud Hands	108
Why?	113
The Graphic Tai Chi Classic	119
Epilogue	128
Acknowledgements	130
Resources	131

Introduction

> *Don't preach at me! I have no love*
> *For images, old gods, or prophetic words.*
> *I want to talk to Utnapishtim!*
> *Tell me how*
>
> - The Epic of Gilgamesh

Why another book, right on the heels of *JUICE Radical Taiji Energetics*? And, is this book merely a recapitulation of the video companion, *Tai Chi PENG Surfing the Soft Wave*? This book differs from its elder brother, JUICE, in three main qualities:

- Traditional
- Focused
- Practical

That's not saying it's *better* – just different.

Traditional: In JUICE, I coined neologisms, cooked up weird acronyms, and played games with the language. I felt it was amusing, and it was my baby version of the 'crazy wisdom' thing where you jolt people by presenting venerable truth in offbeat terms. Some readers didn't agree, but what's the use of a book that merely parrots the same old stuff? Anyway, in this book I use only normal words that will be reassuringly familiar to even the most head-in-the-sand Tai Chi traditionalist.

Focused: The first book was full of incredible anecdotes, hilarious asides, intimate personal memoirs, scathing cultural commentary, scintillating humor, profound quotations ... whereas this book is pretty straight up. It's just the facts (sprinkled with a little glitter here and there).

Practical: JUICE is style independent, and treats broad stuff like mindset and epistemology of internal martial arts, but this book presents working *drills* based on a particular style of Tai Chi – the 37-pose sequence created from the Yang family system by grandmaster Zheng Manqing (ZMQ37). Even in JUICE, I used that as my display window mannequin for examples of a specific pose or practice, but overall JUICE is above the style wars. And so is this book. I just present the work-a-day practice drills that have done the heavy lifting for me, and you can take it or leave it. In any case, there's more hands-on work for your daily routine than you'll find in JUICE, all based on the standard ZMQ37 framework.

This book is more closely aligned with my video: *Tai Chi PENG Surfing the Soft Wave*. The video is also traditional, focused, and practical. But this book isn't merely a blind transcription of the video. Rather, it's a superset, covering more detail on many interesting points than would be possible without doubling the video's length. And though the drills presented here are identical to those on the video, the different format makes it a useful secondary reference for people with different learning styles. Some things I could only touch on in JUICE were expanded and shown graphically in the video, and now in turn, some things I only mentioned briefly in the video are developed further in this book.

I'm still talking about exactly the same thing, in the video and in both books. It's all *one thing*. The different approaches and terminologies (across JUICE, on the one hand, and this PENG book and its companion video on the other) are two fingers pointing at the same moon. I could say they're divergent routes up different faces of the same mountain to a single summit, but even that doesn't go far enough. In fact, all of these materials are talking about exactly the same thing.

In JUICE, I used my own spin on the language of the Taoist energy hierarchy, specifically that of Xingyiquan master Guo Yunshen. With this PENG stuff, I'm sticking to the plain terms of traditional Tai Chi – PENG energy in particular. But the experience of it is consistent either way. It's three things: a *hard wave* transitioning to a *soft wave* that ends in an *empty state* - no matter how you slice it. It isn't two tracks up the same mountain, it's differing *views* of the *same* track and the *same* scenery. It's like photographing that one landscape using ultraviolet, then again using night enhancement, and then again with infrared. Three different-looking pictures result - but they are all one place. There is nowhere else to be.

Tai Chi and PENG Energy

*I'm safe, up high –
You're my protection
No pain, inside –
You're like perfection
But how do I feel this good sober?*

- Pink

What is Tai Chi? Physical fitness, physical therapy, slow motion folk dance, martial art, moving meditation – such is the hand a beginner Tai Chi student is dealt. But I play a single card – Tai Chi is the tool for ramping you to the greatest possible natural high. That's something even a lot of Tai Chi veterans don't much emphasize. Do you enjoy snorting coke, shooting smack, smoking weed? Tai Chi's PENG energy is a natural high that's far beyond all that.

If people understood this, there might be a lot less violence, addiction, depression, and aggression… all those nasty things might be eliminated by deeper understanding of our internal potential. Tai Chi is a tool for cultivating and enjoying the internal energy. It *can* be used for the other things I've listed: as physical therapy, for physical fitness, as dance, for cultural appreciation, as a martial art. But thinking of Tai Chi primarily in those terms is like using a flash memory stick to stir your cocktail. It can be done but it isn't the point.

What is PENG? That Chinese word in the title (rhymes with 'tongue') refers to a wave of fluid energy you'll feel flowing up from your feet and suffusing your entire body, when you practice Tai Chi correctly. It has a hydraulic feel. I call it a non-physical energy, even though you need your physical body to experience it. Actually, it *is* physical, because we need our body to experience it. But it's *non*-physical in that it will *feel* really different from anything else you experience. In JUICE, I call this 'Surge 2' or the *wave* phenomenon. But it can manifest in a variety of ways so I'll talk in detail about how it will feel.

One of the practical points about PENG energy, apart from the sheer ecstasy of it, is that it can protect you. Chen Weiming, a student of the great master Yang Chengfu, and a famous teacher in his own right, wrote:

*The various martial arts produce different energies but Tai Chi is relaxed and loose and produces an energy that is **soft and hard at the same time**. If you practice an external martial art system and don't have relaxed energy, you can be injured in a sudden attack. When you're loose and relaxed, even when not alert, **the energy is still there** and it spreads everywhere. Thus **you cannot be injured**.*

(*T'ai Chi Ch'uan Ta Wen Questions and Answers on T'ai Chi Ch'uan*; Chen Wei-Ming, Benjamin Lo, Robert W. Smith; 1985 Blue Snake Books)

A key phrase there is: *even when you're not alert*. When a famous Tai Chi master was walking in Beijing one day, he was slammed from behind by a large cart which rebounded off him, was hurled across the street, smashed into the opposite wall, and was totally destroyed. The master just kept on walking and talking to his companion. At his extremely high level, that energy was always active in him. His attainment was far beyond any of us. But the story shows the protective potential of the power.

I've experienced this too, even as a teenager with only five years or so Tai Chi under my belt. I once found myself taken for a ride by a paranoid maniac who drove us around the DC beltway at 80 mph, screaming his determination to drive straight through the rail and over the side of the next upcoming bridge, plunging us a hundred feet straight down into the Potomac River. Judging there to be no good options for taking control of the car (a struggle for the wheel would probably have ended in a multi-vehicle pileup, killing all and sundry), I opened the passenger door and jumped out.

I hit the concrete shoulder at eighty miles an hour and was rolled ten times by the momentum. My clothes were completely shredded off. It was the hardest impact I'd ever felt. But the ER doctors who subsequently checked me out said: *This should have killed you! We can't believe your skull's not fractured and your spine's not broken...* Even highly trained professionals die in much less dangerous stunts, despite every safety precaution, as reported by ABC News a few years ago:

> *Canadian labor officials are investigating the Wednesday death of a veteran stuntman on the set of* Exit Wounds, *Steven Seagal's latest action movie. On Aug. 18, the fateful scene called for Chris Lamon, 35, to jump out of the back doors of a van. Lamon, who had been performing dangerous maneuvers for 14 years, allegedly hit his head when he leapt from the moving vehicle. "He made an error with his footing," Warner Bros. Senior Vice President Mark Reina told The Hollywood Reporter. "He landed badly and hit his head on the pavement. We are very sad about this. It doesn't happen very often." The injured stuntman received immediate care on the set by paramedics and was then rushed to St. Michael's Hospital in Toronto, where he was diagnosed with a fractured skull. He died Aug. 23*

Just like Lamon, I also landed head first, slamming the back of my skull on the concrete at first impact. I hadn't yet trained under Russian Systema master Vladimir Vasiliev, and I had no idea how to correctly roll out of a moving vehicle. But I was fine, except for all the abrasions and lacerations. That's because of the PENG energy's automatic protective quality.

In this book I teach you to RIDE the energy. That is: *Recognize*, *Initiate*, *Direct*, and *Extend* it. (Oops! OK, that's the *one* little acronym in this book - for old times' sake.)

The first thing is to *recognize* it. If you don't believe that there is any such energy, then it's not going to happen. You need that little bit of faith to get started. So let's talk in more detail about what PENG energy is and how it manifests.

I like to compare it to water. Water is the primary metaphor of Taoism. PENG energy conforms to a water-like model, because it can be static, like a lake, or can flow like a river or riptide. A flow can be either a continuous stream, or come in waves. And waves are also of two types: the hard breakers on the shore, with whitecaps cresting and breaking, or longer, slower, smoother and much more powerful ocean swells that don't break for hundreds of miles. Eventually you can feel the PENG energy in all these modes.

I've used a surfing metaphor on the cover of the companion video, because for one thing, surfing involves water, our basic Taoist symbol. Secondly, ocean waves represent a force that's beyond us. We don't control that force, but we can learn to merge with it and have some fun along the way.

I'm not a great surfer but I've been surfing a few times in Hawaii. Surfing can't be taught. You just see other people doing it and from picking up a few expert hints you figure it out. I'm going to give you more than a few hints, but the key thing is that you have to try it yourself. To be motivated to try it, you have to believe it's something worth doing. With surfing, *that* part's easy – the guys look cool out there. But Tai Chi PENG training is internal, invisible. So you'll have to make that leap of faith, decide: *maybe this guy knows something he can show me* - and then try it on your own. Once you get a taste of the energy, there'll be no stopping you.

Song of PENG

Wake me up inside

- Evanescence

JUICE contains all the theoretical and conceptual background on this energy, presents some traditional touchstones, and gives many practical hints. But I didn't present there the exercises that I show in this book. That's because JUICE is universal. Everything in JUICE applies to all styles of Tai Chi, of which there are many. I didn't want to limit it to one particular style. The exercises here are drawn from ZMQ37 Tai Chi, which is the main type I've studied for forty years. Although I've also trained most of the other major branches, I've found ZMQ37 to be the best fit to my interest in energy cultivation and deployment. In JUICE I didn't want to push that point quite so heavily.

The ancient Chinese text compendium on Tai Chi is called the *Tai Chi Classic Writings* (they really aren't all that ancient, dating mostly from the 18th and 19th centuries, but they reflect much earlier ideas). These materials clearly show that the ancient Chinese experienced and understood PENG energy. Their word for it - 掤 (péng) - is sometimes translated as 'wardoff', a kind of repelling or bouncing type of power. We'll use a section of the *Classics* that defines PENG as our touchstone and benchmark. With this text in hand, we'll know whether sensations arising in our practice are taking us farther from, or closer to, what these great masters had in mind.

The *Song of PENG* is called a song because it's metrically structured, in the old fashioned Chinese writing style. They didn't actually sing it. Let's go through the Chinese text, with my original translation and comments.

掤勁義何解 *How can peng energy be explained?*

This is the standard opening for a new topic in the old-fashioned writing style.

如水負行舟 *It's like the swelling water that lifts a boat.*

In the line above, you can see they noticed that water is the perfect metaphor. The gentle and yet irresistible power of water is what you'll feel. I've experienced precisely this hydraulic quality.

先實丹田氣 *First, fill the dantian with qi,*

The *dantian* is the energy accumulation center in the lower abdomen, a few inches below the navel. Many martial artists know the importance of this area. You can learn to feel this spot; it's not a metaphor or an abstract symbol. *Qi* is the universal energy that comes from air, food, and water – everything we interact with. It's our life energy. But strangely enough, *qi* is not PENG. The *qi* is the feedstock. It can be refined, strengthened, and transformed into functional PENG energy. We all have *qi* energy, but not everyone is able to recognize and manipulate the PENG energy.

次要頂頭懸 *then, hold the head in light suspension.*

Here they are talking about relaxing the head and neck, and keeping some mental awareness in that area of your body.

全體彈簧力 *A tensile, elastic power suffuses the entire body,*

Water has an elastic quality. If you push an inflatable toy down in the bath, it'll pop up again.

開合一定間 *oscillating at a fixed frequency.*

They're talking about energy here. Energy is often represented as an alternation, as a signal or current alternating between two states, expressed as positive/negative amplitude (in a sine wave) or open/closed in a filtered or impulse system. I'm sure you've seen many forced and awkward translations for this line, simply because most translators haven't felt the juice. This line doesn't refer to any specific combative physical/kinetic gesture. The first two characters mean *'opening closing'*, which has led translators to assume it's about physical technique. But (to cite one of many possible examples) the quintessential case of a periodic (acoustic) energy wave signal is the human voice. Voicing in speech or song is produced by the rapid 'opening' and 'closing' action of the glottal folds. The literary Chinese language didn't provide the necessary vocabulary to write technically as we now do about frequencies and periodic signals, so this is how they expressed it, using the word 間 which here means *interval*. Thus in this context, the line refers to frequency of a periodic or wave energy.

任有千斤重 *Even a thousand pounds of force...*

飄浮亦不難 *will be easily repelled.*

Here they probably had in mind something like the incident of the heavy cart colliding in the street with the Tai Chi master, as discussed previously.

That is the succinct classical definition of the PENG energy. But other understandings of the term PENG exist in the Tai Chi community. Let's walk through a couple of alternatives.

First, in all Tai Chi styles, there are certain fundamental postures, named body positions. One of them is *peng* or 'wardoff' posture. In most styles it entails holding an arm out in front of your chest horizontally as you brace your rear foot strongly.

You have your arm out in a kind of warding-off motion, and you're holding a fixed front-weighted stance. There is *zuo peng* with the left leg forward, and *you peng* with the right leg forward. This is merely a physical position, but it uses the same name as the *energy* we just saw discussed in the Song of PENG.

However, a posture per se is not a form of energy. In the Song of PENG, they are talking about a dynamic energy, about a 'spring-like quality'. The Song of PENG also uses the metaphor of water – so again, a physical posture cannot be the correct interpretation. I won't ever tell you: *PENG is when you take such-and-such a pose and you throw somebody far away.* That's a very superficial understanding and it has nothing to do with what I'll be talking about here. It's merely a coincidental overlap of terms. You can have just as much PENG energy suffusing your body when you're just standing around at the bus stop as you do when demonstrating a perfect *peng* pose on stage for an audience of thousands.

Yet another alternative way to think about PENG is that it's *mechanical bracing*. Suppose you take the *peng* posture (though the principle can be applied to any posture). When people show this they usually straighten or strengthen their rear leg, and say: *This is the embodiment of peng energy, because if someone pushed here on my arm, their push would go straight into my root and they wouldn't be able to move me.*

That is also not what I'll be talking about here. That is a mechanical effect, requiring that you align your bones, muscles, fascia tissues, tendons, and ligaments just so. As long as you hold that configuration, it may be hard for somebody smaller than yourself, or even slightly larger, to move you with a direct shove. If you deviate from that pose, you'll open yourself to charges of the dreaded *incorrect structure* disability.

Here's what a hypothetical Tai Chi teacher might espouse:

Tai Chi PENG

The power is in the structure, not in any effort I'm using to resist his pressure. So his hard push goes into my arm and straight down through my back, through the ground, and into the earth. As long as I maintain that alignment with the ground, I'm ok. My body offers no resistance and no tension. My structure is aligned with the ground, so I have what is called peng jing which is like water supporting a boat. As he pushes, he just floats on me. I can push him using that same structure, using the stabilizing muscles in my body, without using force, with just a small movement.

That's a typical summation of this condition where you line up your body mechanically and use your 'stabilizing muscles' to either push someone or resist their push. All of that has nothing to do with the PENG energy as defined in the Song of PENG. The PENG energy is independent of any particular posture, and independent of all muscles, stabilizing or otherwise. It is a non-physical energy that merely manifests through the body. It is *in* the body but not *of* or *from* the body.

If you hold to the mechanical/structural understanding of PENG, you are turning your body into a door security bar, a metal brace that costs $20 at Home Depot. When jammed under a doorknob, it will keep any door closed by transferring all incoming pressure to the ground. Is that what the Song of PENG is pointing at?

A spring-like power suffuses the entire body... oscillating at a fixed frequency... like the surge of water that lifts a boat.

Though the door bar may give one micrometer or so, it definitely isn't water-like. This book has nothing to do with this common (mis)understanding of PENG.

Another problem with interpreting PENG as either a posture or a mechanical principle turns up when we ask ourselves: *what kind of martial art requires that you always maintain a certain configuration of*

Figure 1: A door brace effortlessly transfers force directly to the ground

your body? That's an unrealistic condition. It might have some small drill value but not much more than that. I trained for a decade with the Russian Systema master Vladimir Vasiliev. He told us things like this:

You may have to fight in a drainpipe, in a garbage dumpster, in a car or beneath a tank. You may get picked up entirely, off the ground. Or your arms and legs might be restrained by cuffs, or gripped by multiple attackers.

What would it mean to insist: *I must brace like the door bar in order to deploy my combative power?* Clearly the authors of the Song of PENG, who were great fighting masters, were talking about something else.

Each section of the book will cover one aspect of PENG, culminating in the energetic practice drills. First I explain the energetic architecture of the body, then I present the exercises in stages. First, I introduce the body's energetic architecture as it relates to the experience and daily practice of PENG cultivation through Tai Chi. Then, because we'll need a bit of physical structure to ground the energy, I present seven basic and essential poses extracted from the ZMQ37 form. These can be performed with maximum relaxation by means of the unique 'assisted relaxation' protocol. Finally, the 'expanding post' method of energy extension throughout the body is illustrated for each of the seven test poses.

Energetic Architecture

*If you want to find the secrets of the universe,
think in terms of energy, frequency and vibration.*

- Nikola Tesla

I'm going to talk about the body's energetic architecture – but strictly as it relates to the PENG energy development. Much more could be said about acupuncture and Chinese medicine. The ancient Chinese hypothesized a complicated energy anatomy made up of thousands of meridians and energy hotspots. But for Tai Chi PENG, we don't need to know all that. So I'm going to streamline it, because all we care about is getting that PENG feeling, the underfoot buoyancy, lifting straight through the body. If somebody takes a drug, they don't care how it was manufactured, or how the neurochemicals work, they want that hit, the high.

The poem presented below, like the Song of PENG introduced earlier, is from the 19th century Tai Chi Classics. This segment is not usually included in the English translations of the Tai Chi Classics that you find in any bookstore. This one is more obscure. But it's the most directly aligned with my purpose. And though it isn't so well known to the Western Tai Chi community, it's all over the Chinese internet. I'll step through it in some detail to show that these Tai Chi masters explicitly recognized the energy pathway. It's not mysterious or abstract. But neither is it mechanically structured like so much Tai

Chi of the present day. It describes precisely what I've experienced in my own practice.

神氣運行歌

The Song of Qi and Spirit Energy Deployment

氣如長江水, 滔滔向東流

Qi power is like the eastward-surging Yangzi River torrent

Here again we have the masters using water imagery. That's our best clue that PENG is not a mechanical phenomenon, it's a fluid energy.

來自湧泉穴, 路經脊背過

Starting from the foot's bubbling well point, rising up through the spinal channel

The master who wrote this talks about the route the energy takes through the body. It's going to originate from the sole of the foot, transit to the palms of the hands and finally spread out to the fingers. It's transmitted through the entire body. We're going to start from the sole of the foot and work up, and then down, through the points he mentions. Many of these points were presented in JUICE. In the line above, he's talking about the *yongquan*, a point on the sole of the foot, on the centerline and bit back from the front ridge behind the toes.

In my experience, it isn't really necessary or helpful to particularly emphasize this point, as opposed to the entire sole of the foot (felt as a unitary surface). If you think of the entire sole as the origin, you'll be good to go. We want to keep the inventory of points to an absolute minimum, because over-focus on them, or on any particular one, can lead to tension - exactly what we don't want. As we'll see later, relaxation is key. So I think of the line above as talking about the *sole* of the foot rather than the *yongquan* per se. But either way is doable. The electric current hits every bulb on the wire of a Christmas tree light string.

Either way, the energy begins at the foot. It begins most particularly in the "strong" or substantial foot (this concept will be explained in detail), and will usually be experienced by beginners as rising from the heel along the back of the leg (relaxing the instep in the front part of the ankle helps to kick-start the process). It continues through several important energy points up through the lower and mid back, which form the lower part of the spinal channel.

來到泥丸宮, 回到印堂闕

Continuing upward to the niwan center, then lowering into the brow point

The *niwan* point is the center of the brain. Often in Tai Chi people talk about the crown point (*baihui*) on the top of the head, but that's very hard to feel. The *niwan* is the true energy intake and control center for the whole system. The author of this obscure segment of the Tai Chi Classics has confirmed this explicitly right here. Though it isn't mentioned in most of the other writings that make up the standard Classics, this master, obviously writing from personal experience, really nailed it.

From the *niwan*, the energy projects forward (lowers into) the brow point or *yintang*. This is sometimes called the 'third eye' in other traditions. Here the energy isn't merely stringing along to just another 'point'. It's projecting from the *niwan* in a *fanout* across the entire brow and forehead area. You'll feel the stream of energy projecting forward from the center of the brain all over the surface of the forehead.

心意將氣領，從不稍離別

The mind leads the qi, the two never diverging even slightly

In this line, he's giving general advice. You use your mind to direct the energy, just as a seamstress leads a thread with a needle.

譬如右拳舉，意氣到手腋

Let's say the right hand prepares to strike, the mind directs the qi to the armpit

Now he's going to give us an example of energy projection. So far we've talked about the energy *rising*, from the feet and legs, up the back, and across the head to the brow area. This rising process is commonly emphasized in other traditions, such as yoga and various forms of meditation. You often hear about *kundalini rising* and so on.

Now, this author introduces the *outward/downward* path, which is less commonly discussed but relevant to martial arts. There is a YouTube video clip: *Cheng Man Ching discusses Chi*. This is Zheng Manqing speaking through an interpreter about how hard it is to *raise* the energy (to the *niwan*) and saying that subsequently, it's relatively easy to *drop* the energy to and through the hands, for martial arts. In JUICE, apart from presenting one key energy hotspot, I didn't go into great detail on the outward phase, but this author covers the whole process.

Remember, as of the previous line, we have the rising phase activating the brow and forehead areas. The energy will then lower to the armpits. Eventually you'll feel the armpit point, where the arm joins the upper/side chest (*yuanye*), pulsing with the flow.

隨勁意氣到，覺之在肘窩

The mind manifests the qi as palpable internal power through the crook of the elbow

Here the outward phase continues. You'll feel the energy bubbling through the crook of the inner elbow.

順勢一反拳, 意氣到內關穴

As the hand turns upward, the mind guides the qi power through the inner wrist

I'm translating the acupoint term *neiguan* as *inner wrist*. It's essentially the same key concept I covered in JUICE, but there I focused on the *daling* point, where the hand and forearm join, whereas the *neiguan* is the neighboring point slightly up toward the elbow. Though *all* points will light up from the energy current, I have found in my own practice that using the *daling* as the major mental relay station in the forearm gives the strongest charge. But as with everything in this book: *play around with it and find what works best for you.* Don't worry, the energy won't bite.

右拳前按出, 掌心微突越

When the right hand pushes out, the palm center bulges slightly

Some great masters can show the skin of the palm center bulging up and out like an old fashioned popcorn cooker. The tinfoil pan cover rises up in a dome shape when heated.

氣經掌陰面, 直到五指尖

The qi energy, passing across the surface of the inner hand, directly charges the five fingers

When the energy hits your hands, your fingertips will feel puffed up like bubble wrap, the little plastic packaging bubbles that come in sheets. This means you have activated the entire circuit, from the sole of your foot to your fingers.

A possibly confusing phenomenon of the energy rise phase is that when the energy reaches the mid back point, between the shoulder blades (*lingtai*) it continues to rise through the head and *niwan* as described. However, you'll *also* feel it branching sideways across the back to the shoulders, flowing into the arms from there. Despite that, the energy must go through the head for its full expression. We don't want to short-circuit it at the *lingtai*, thinking *Why do I need to talk about my head in this game?* The energy must filter through the head for the fully refined power to emerge.

Energy Hotspots

I've talked about the feeling of flow that you'll get. Now I'll add a little information about each of the points on the energy line. But just because I limit the discussion to these dozen or so points, that doesn't mean the others don't exist or don't matter. Remember, when the current starts in the Christmas tree light string, every bulb is hit, all the way to the end. It's a continuous current so you'll feel all the points. But it's useful to single out certain points for extra concentration, especially in the beginning, before your body's every cell has been totally permeated by the power.

The list below includes all points that are discussed explicitly and emphasized in JUICE, together with all the points mentioned in the *Song of Qi and Spirit Energy Deployment* (text covered in previous section).

DANTIAN   丹田   dāntián

The *dantian* is where energy accumulates from all sources, not just from rigorous meditative training, but from what you eat, what you breathe, what you see… everything that happens to you, or that you perceive, is bouncing around your body in energetic form. If you do the Tai Chi practice correctly, all that begins to coalesce in the *dantian*, and the lower abdominal area. That's the starting point for this whole process.

It's also the end point. The full energy cycle presented in JUICE both begins and ends with the energy buzzing and humming in your relaxed *dantian*; feeling like you have a radioactive beehive down there.

FEET

If you relax your upper body enough, that coalescence of random energies from all over will drop to your feet. That moment is where the process of this book really begins.

YONGQUAN 涌泉 yǒngquán

The *Song of Qi and Spirit Energy Deployment* emphasizes this particular point on the sole of the foot.

DANTIAN 丹田 dāntián

We just talked about the *dantian*, why has it come up again? I talked about dropping energy from the *dantian* to the feet. Subsequently, the *dantian* refills *from below*. That's an amazing sensation that tells you you're really getting somewhere. You'll feel the energy come from the soles of the feet, up through your legs, and then it surges up into, not only the *dantian*, but the entire area of the lower hips and abdomen. That's the beginning of the upward process. So the *dantian* is again important, when the energy comes back around.

LINGTAI 靈台 língtái

The *lingtai* is the point between the shoulder blades. This is the branch point, where the energy both goes sideways to the arms and also begins to rise to the head. In the Classic he doesn't mention the *lingtai* explicitly, as a point per se. He talks simply about the *spinal channel*, which contains many points along its length. But I emphasize the *lingtai* because you can really feel it. This is the first of our 'projective' points, a concept I explain just below.

NIWAN 泥丸 níwán

The *niwan* is the head center point. This is mentioned both in JUICE and also by the author of the Classic. It's mentioned explicitly by both

Scott Meredith

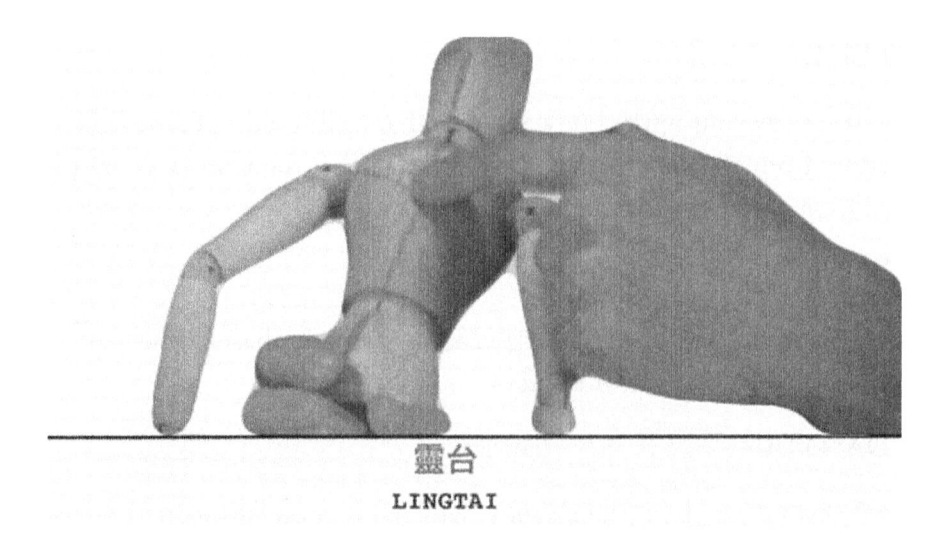

靈台
LINGTAI

Figure 2: The *lingtai* is the point between the shoulder blades

of us because this is the most important point of all. This is the control center. When the energy reaches that point in the brain, you can put it from there anywhere you want in your body. But the default path is to continue into the *yintang*, the brow point.

I need to backup up a minute and explain that three of these points have special properties. That's why three in particular are emphasized over all others in JUICE. The *lingtai*, the *niwan*, and the *daling* (inner wrist point) all have a *projective* property.

In old movie theaters they had the film projector at the back. It threw out a light beam that filled the entire screen in front. If you looked back from your seat, you could see the narrow beam emerging from the projection booth and fanning out to cover the big screen. Most of our energy points don't have that property; they're merely like the Christmas tree bulbs. But these three (*lingtai, niwan, daling*) fan out.

For example, from the *niwan*, the energy doesn't just go straight to the brow point, it fans out across the forehead. Likewise, from the *daling*, the energy doesn't only go straight to the inner palm point (*laogong*). It fans out into the entire hand. Likewise the back point doesn't only go straight up to the *niwan*, it fans out. So those three points are what I call projective points. I emphasize these because when it projects, you have a better chance to feel it more directly.

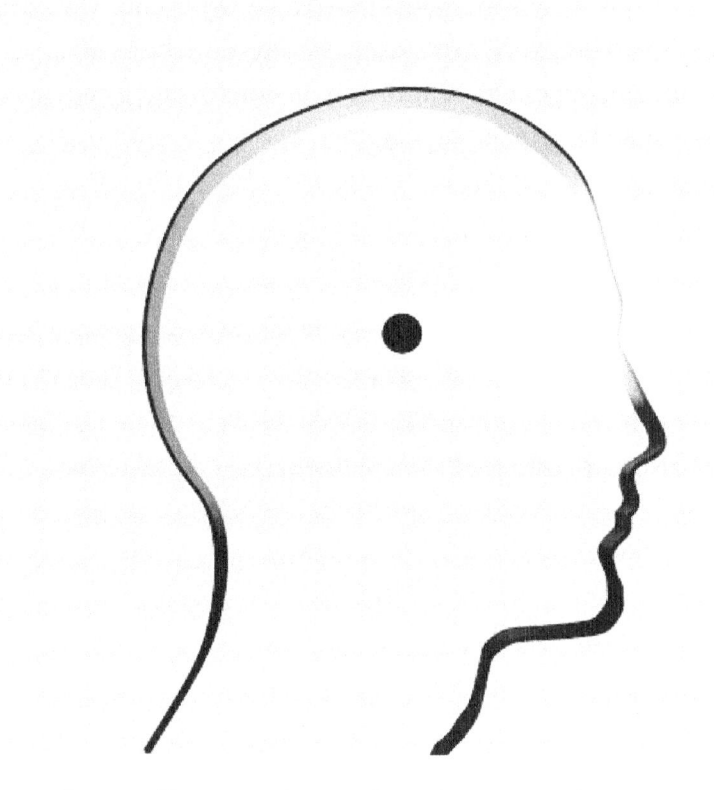

Figure 3: The energy fans out from the *niwan* to the *yintang* area

YINTANG　　印堂　　yìntáng

The *yintang* has already been covered, as the center of an expansive generation from the *niwan* center.

YUANYE　　泉液　　yuānyè

Scott Meredith

NEIGUAN 內關 nèiguān
DALING 大陵 dàling

The above three points function together as the power source threading through the arms for internal martial arts. Of course, in martial arts we need not be constrained to strike or work only with arms. Legs, feet, hips, shoulders, head, even the chest can be used to strike, jam, or submit an opponent. But the discussions of energy circulation in the *Classics* focus on the arm channels because if you can generate the energy in a clear channel all the way from feet to fingers, you have no blockage. You can easily put the energy anywhere else, such as the body areas just cited, for combative use.

The armpit point, *yuanye*, is interesting. Zheng Manqing stated in his book *Zheng-zi Taijiquan Zi Xiu Xin Fa*, (鄭子太極拳自修新法) that one night he dreamed both his arms were broken. When he awoke, he felt his arms had achieved the quality of Tai Chi relaxation called *song*.

Here's his exact wording and a literal word-by-word translation of this famous Tai Chi quotation:

忽夢覺兩臂已斷

sudden dream feel two arms broke/separated

醒驚試之

awaken surprise try it

恍然悟得鬆境

amazed realized get relax condition

Figure 4: The *daling* point is where the hand and forearm meet

In the next day's training session, he defeated all his usual tough senior classmates using that new quality. From then on, he was considered a Tai Chi master.

The key word in the quotation is: 斷 duàn. The Collins Chinese-English Dictionary defines this word in two senses:

1. verb [分成段] break

2. verb [斷絕] break ... off

When people cite this quotation, they are usually assuming he meant the first sense, an ordinary arm break - like a skiing accident. But having experienced this energy flowing through the armpit point, I believe what he actually meant was the *second* sense, that of something breaking or dropping *off*, separating.

It's as though after the dream, *he had no arms*, meaning nowhere remained for tension to accumulate. That interpretation coheres with the sense of freedom and looseness you get from the PENG energy really streaming out through your arms fully. So his arms became free, almost feeling independent of his body.

The idea of arms 'breaking *off*' or 'separating from' rather than merely 'breaking' can be well visualized with damaged classical statuary, as below. The break point is almost exactly at the *yuanye*.

The *neiguan* and *daling* are both in the inner wrist area. The *daling* is easy to locate because it's right at the edge where the base of the palm meets the forearm. The *neiguan* is a few centimeters "up" from there, toward the elbow. The author of the Classic has chosen to single out the *neiguan* in his account of the energy stream. This is perfectly valid, by the principle of the Christmas tree bulb string. Everything lights up. In JUICE, I emphasized the neighboring *daling* point because that's easier for beginners to feel. The *daling* is also the foundation of the traditional yet mysterious Yang family teaching about the importance of "settling" or "setting" the wrists in Tai Chi form practice.

FINGERTIPS

The endpoint of all this is your fingertips, which will feel like bubble wrap when you do this stuff right.

This energy going through the points can be experienced as either a *state* (simultaneous activation of all these points) - or it can be experienced as a *flow*. The flow can be either continuous or alternating (a sine wave type of feeling). Water also has those three modes.

Figure 5: The *yuanye* point is exactly at the underside juncture of the arm and shoulder

Remember that *all* points will light up in this process. For example, in the discussion above I skip over the stretch between the *yintang* (brow area) and the *yuanye* (armpit). But of course the *jing* energy will flow through everything in between. For some people, it may be helpful to learn and mentally engage those points. Unconscious tension held in any of the intermediate areas will affect the overall soles-to-fingers activation. Conscious probing of those points with your mind can identify blocks.

In the given example, between the brow and armpit the point at the base of the throat will be traversed. That is *Heaven Rushing Out* (Conception Vessel 22), located at the base of the throat in the large hollow directly below the Adam's apple – and it will really throb like crazy when you get the energy running. But never lock your focus on any intermediate point for very long. The goal is your hands. Eyes on the prize!

Finally, the energy returns to the *dantian* where it began. I know it seems weird – we just talked about the energy being expressed through the hands. How did the *dantian* get back into it, now for the third time? It's like an electric circuit. Electrical machines are hooked into a circuit, a complete circle of electrical current. The motor just "borrows" some of the electrons that flow through on their way back to a negative pole. The *dantian* serves as both positive and negative pole on the body's battery, both source and sink.

The current always flows through the entire circuit, even when you can't feel it directly as such. Later when your *dantian* area and entire lower abdomen are really relaxed, then you'll only have to put your awareness to your *dantian* for an instant, and you'll feel the charge leap directly to your hands. In fact, it's always completing the entire circuit just discussed.

But you must practice *relaxing* that whole *dantian* / lower abdomen area. I don't know why this zone seems to be so tough to relax. Don't focus on the *dantian* as a *point* so much as an *area* – the whole lower belly, or in Chinese: 氣海 (qìhǎi) 'Sea of *qi*'. Keep that area as soft as tofu – be water, not ice. It seems that most people are really hard - right where Tai Chi needs us to be our softest. Is it because our culture teaches us to suck in our gut, or because we all secretly want 6-pack abs?

Finally, this is as good a place as any to talk about *sensations*. Sensations in internal martial arts are a controversial subject. Some kickass fighters are natural athletes who've never felt the internal energy sensations. They tend to take a hard line on it, saying *Your level is what you can do, not what you can feel*. I'm sympathetic to this, as far as it goes. We all know bliss bunny types who astral project to Jupiter on a regular basis but can't do anything useful. Certainly you aren't going to blast somebody into next week with the little buzzes and tingles you get from a weekend Qi Gong intensive.

But in a deeper sense, for those who are absolutely dedicated to pursuit of the highest energy mastery, I emphatically reject the premise that sensations don't matter. You *must* pay attention to small, subtle internal signs as breadcrumbs guiding you to the bigger stuff. In engineering that is known as an *objective function*, a guiding evaluative criterion.

In this case, it's a *subjective* function but it can still be kept consistent and useful within yourself. Of course, don't be a fool who assumes he's attained *satori* when somebody flips the light switch in his dark meditation room. Always be suspiciously pondering alternate explanations for anything you experience. At the same time, when you really get the river of this stuff flowing, you'll understand that it's impossible to have the energy running full bore and not feel it happening. It's just that real.

Anybody who thinks s/he can achieve high mastery without any sensations, without feeling anything strikingly unusual, needs to re-read Sun Lutang's amazing personal testimony that I translated and included in JUICE as Appendix A: *Are You Experienced*. There he writes that when he and his classmates first began to experience the mysterious transformative energy, they weren't willing to reveal what they *felt*, because outsiders wouldn't have the remotest idea what they were talking about. Later he opened up more on what he called *inner information* (內中消息).

Read Sun's first-hand report and tell me that Sun could have somehow attained his superb *level* while avoiding all the *sensations* he details there. I'm certain that every one of the truly great internal masters felt sensations which, if they occurred spontaneously in an unprepared and untrained person, would melt the victim straight down through the floorboards. As long as what you feel seems roughly consistent with what the greatest masters have written, assume you're on the right track and seek more and better of the same.

Practice Principles

> *The Master said:*
> *In archery, piercing the target is not the essential,*
> *for men are not of equal strength.*
>
> - Analects of Confucius

I will present seven poses taken from the Zheng Manqing style of Tai Chi as the foundation for the energy work. They must be done in a certain way, according to the guidelines that I'll explain. But remember, we don't want to get too hung up on the poses themselves. Because they're physical, something we can see and feel, it's easy to believe that the postures per se are the point of the exercise.

But they aren't the point at all. People want to feel strong and beautiful. The physical aspects of the discipline may seem to be a route to those shallow objectives. But here, we're working on energy, and the physicality of the postures is always subordinate. Though it's natural to grope toward either of the two most typical mis-directions (the *mechanical* and the *aesthetic*) – don't do that.

The postures involve physical structure. We'll be doing things with our bodies. But even beneficial structure entails tension. The prime pre-requisite is the *removal* of tension. Relaxation is the number one principle. These poses, and the structure and tension they bring in, are an artificial device. We hope it's only a little bit of tension. In medicine, a small dose cures and an overdose kills. The great Indian sage Ramana Maharishi said if you get a thorn in your foot while walking in the jungle, you grab another thorn to dig it out – then throw both away. Once you have the energy streaming, you don't need any structure.

The postures I'll introduce are like a pointing finger - but we just want to see the moon. If somebody points out the moon, and you, looking only at the finger, say, *That isn't well manicured* or *That's not a very beautiful finger*, then you're completely missing the point.

That said, these postures have only ever been perfectly demonstrated by one man, the founding creator of this system, Professor Zheng Manqing. There are books with photographs of the Professor performing all these postures. The 'Resources' section at the end of this book has their publication information. Fortunately, you don't need perfect postures to make this work.

Let's return to surfing for a moment. To get your ride going, you have to paddle out (which is totally exhausting) and then, once you time into a likely wave, you've got to struggle up onto your board – and only then do you *ride*. Performing these postures is like those first two elements of surfing. Though many people assume Tai Chi *is* the postures and the transitions between them, those things are only the paddleout, not the ride.

Here are the principles of Tai Chi practice:

身正體鬆　　*Upright relaxed body*

The upper body is usually upright and straight while doing these training poses. In real martial arts applications, your body is freely configured. Like water, you do whatever's necessary to fit the situation. But for training, one of the principles is to keep your body upright most of the time, and relaxed all the time. While relaxation is the most essential pre-requisite, keep in mind that PENG energy cultivation, rather than relaxation for its own sake, is the ultimate goal.

Relaxation obviously isn't any kind of rigid muscular tension. It's a natural, effortless state. But it isn't total loosening of everything to the point that you fall onto the floor. That apparent total relaxation is actually *collapse*. Collapse is indeed complete muscular relaxation, but in that state you've sacrificed your mind. That's like being asleep or drunk – your mind is gone. We want to keep our mind aware and alert while removing any unnecessary physical tension. The perfect state between rigidity and collapse is *relaxed*.

沈肩垂肘　　*Sink shoulders and elbows*

People's elbows and shoulders tend to ride up due to tension in daily life. But when we train these poses, we need to keep the elbows and shoulders feeling as though they're sinking slightly. Just as a feeling though – don't force them down.

Yang Chengfu wrote:

沈肩者, 肩鬆開下垂也, 若不能鬆垂, 兩肩端起, 則氣亦隨之而上, 全身皆不得力矣 墜肘者, 肘往下鬆墜之意, 肘若懸起, 則肩不能沈, 放人不遠, 近於外家之斷勁矣

The shoulders should be relaxed and open. Being unable to relax and sink means the two shoulders will rise and tense up. The qi will follow them up, leaving your whole body powerless. "Drop the elbows" means the elbows go down and relax. If the elbows rise, the shoulders won't sink and you cannot blast people to any great distance. The blast will then amount to little more than the fragmented energy of the external methods.

尾閭中正　　*Straighten lower back*

In all these poses, we never want a ducktail effect, where our butt is sticking out. The lower back should be hanging straight down, flat as a chopping block. The tailbone is almost tucked in (but without exaggerating that, to the detriment of the 'upright body' principle).

呼吸自然   *Breathe naturally*

This one often confuses people, because there are so many complex breathing regimens out there. Many people know of yogic *ujjayi* breathing and breath of fire, and there's reverse breathing and *pranayama* of every imaginable description. These are elaborate and rigid forms of breath control, that may have benefits for many purposes, but they aren't relevant to the gradual organic development of Tai Chi PENG energy. In this Tai Chi work, we will always breathe naturally.

美人手   *Fair Lady's Hand*

This hand shape is unique to the ZMQ style of Tai Chi. You won't find it discussed in other styles of Tai Chi, but it's very important for the energy work. The term is based on ancient Chinese thinking that a lovely lady would never have an ugly or distorted shape of hand. A well-bred lady would keep her hands softly extended and conservatively configured at all times. Fair Lady's Hand means straight but not stiff. You can understand it simply by gently resting your forearm, from elbow to fingertips, against a wall. The natural shape that you assume when you slightly draw your arm down the wall is the Fair Lady's Hand shape.

It isn't the 'sword hand' or *te-gatana* that you see other styles of martial arts, because that tends to be rigid. In Fair Lady's Hand, there's a very slight natural curve at the wrist, and all the fingers are aligned forward and straight. You don't stick out your thumb or take on any other shape.

分清虛實   *Distinguish substantial/insubstantial*

Tai Chi PENG

This one could also be understood as 'distinguish yin/yang'. Yin/yang are Chinese philosophical terms describing pairs of complementary opposites like night/day, male/female, sun/moon, etc. In Tai Chi, our ears sometimes glaze over when we hear this, taking it as just another abstraction. *That's just how those guys used to talk.* But this is the most important principle, next to relaxation itself. I'll be examining it in greater detail in later chapters. For now, I'll just point out that the meaning of this abstraction – *distinguish substantial from insubstantial* – is going to be cashed out concretely through the *legs*. In every pose, a stronger, fully supporting leg, called *substantial*, will always be differentiated from a weaker or *insubstantial* leg.

Notice that when Yang Chengfu treated this principle, he explicitly cited the legs:

太極拳術以分虛實為第一義，如全身皆坐在右腿，

則右腿為實，左腿為虛，全身皆坐在左腿，

則左腿為實，右腿為虛 虛實能分，

而後轉動輕靈，毫不費力，如不能分，

則邁步重滯，自立不穩，而易為人所牽動

Differentiating between insubstantial and substantial is the first principle in Taijiquan. If the weight of the whole body is resting on the right leg, then the right leg is substantial and the left leg is insubstantial, and vice versa. When you can separate substantial and insubstantial, you can turn lightly without exerting strength. If you cannot separate, the step is heavy and slow. The stance is not firm and you'll be easily toppled by an opponent.

The *Tai Chi Classic Writings* also state: 偏沈則隨，雙重則滯 meaning: *the flow of movement originates on a single side; if you're double-weighted you'll feel stagnant and rigid* and also: 如自己有不得力處，

便是双重未化 meaning: *if you feel any areas of weakness in yourself, it's due to being sluggishly double-weighted.*

意識放長　*Extend consciousness*

You could extend your consciousness to Grand Central Station, or anywhere you want. But for the purposes of this work, it's enough if you can extend your consciousness into your own limbs. What I mean by limbs is fingers, feet, and even your head. If we can extend our consciousness beyond the inner channel of energy circulation (*xiaozhoutian*), which is centered on the spine, then we're beginning to set the foundation for the PENG energy development.

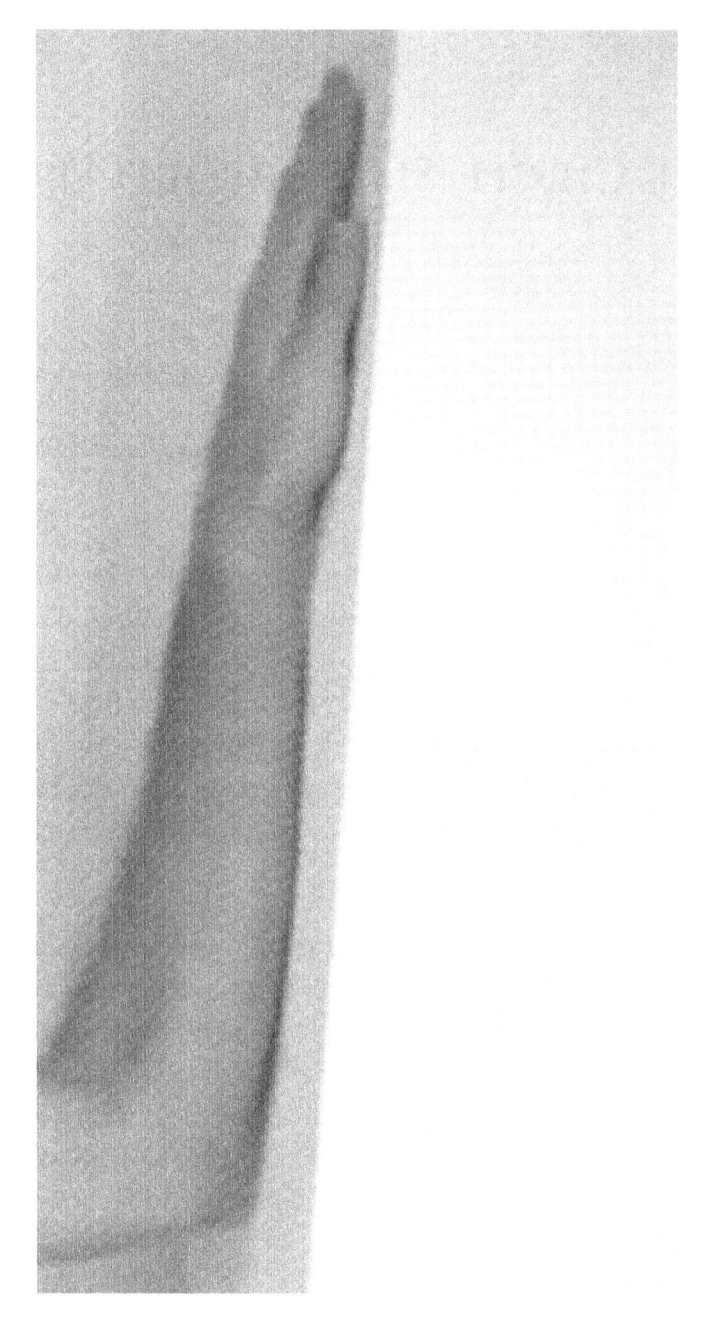

Figure 6: Find 'Fair Lady's Hand' by aligning with a wall

The Circle-Slice Sword Drill

*And show to dust, that is a little gilt,
More laud than gilt o'er dusted*

- William Shakespeare

The energy track outlined in this book is oriented to *cultivation*. For *deployment* of energy (martial arts or healing) mobilization needs to be quick and effortless. A great way to understand the immediate direct link from *dantian* straight to your arms/hands (like a squeezed accordion) is to work with the ZMQ Tai Chi sword form. From that you can easily feel the compressed version of the connection, then transfer it to the empty-hand set, or beyond Tai Chi altogether, into daily life.

If you lack access to a qualified instructor, it will be difficult to learn the full ZMQ sword form, which though not lengthy is a string of complex and subtle movements with fanciful titles like *Rhinoceros Gazes at the Moon* and *White Ape Proffers Fruit*. The mastery of Tai Chi sword performance is a substantial undertaking, requiring the entirety of one or more full human incarnations. I, however, care little for *aesthetics* and *mechanics*, remaining free to focus on my one thing: the energy.

Fortunately there is an extremely simple yet incredibly effective Tai Chi sword drill that offers exactly what we seek – an overwhelming

Tai Chi PENG

energy harvest from an easy movement pattern. Yet this powerful drill, which for optimization of the harvest-to-hassle ratio is nearly unbeatable, is rarely taught and seldom seen. Maybe it's just too starkly simple. Sakyamuni said *the eyes hunger for color, the ears hunger for sound,* so maybe that's the problem? This mousy little drill doesn't make the grade for flash, but it'll blow you away if you give it half a chance.

Essentially it consists of a flat, semi-circular cut across the body, back and forth, really easy and very pleasant to perform. But this drill will shoot the energy through your arms to your hands like nobody's business. If you practice this for 5 or 10 minutes prior to each day's performance of the regular Tai Chi empty hand routine, your arms will eventually throb and pulse with energy like radioactive chainsaws. Don't take it lightly just because it looks so straight-forward.

All the previously discussed Tai Chi principles apply to this exercise so I won't restate them all here. Go back and review all the principles before beginning this drill. But one of our principles, the Fair Lady's Hand, needs a bit of customization for the sword. Obviously you need to grip the sword (use your dominant hand, or you can practice holding the sword in both hands alternately, a few minutes in each hand). The main gripping strength is in the middle finger, with the others just helping to stabilize. Don't grip too tightly, just enough to insure full control of the weapon.

Your off hand should be in the classical *sword pointing fingers* configuration. This may have had some traditional combative function involving *dianxue* (point striking), but I don't care about that. What it's incredibly useful for is mind and energy control. It's an arbitrary shape that's perfect for the dual requirement: *keeping your mind awake at the wheel, yet with minimal physical strain and tension.* Pure genius.

The sword drill's effectiveness lies in the fact that it forces your mind to

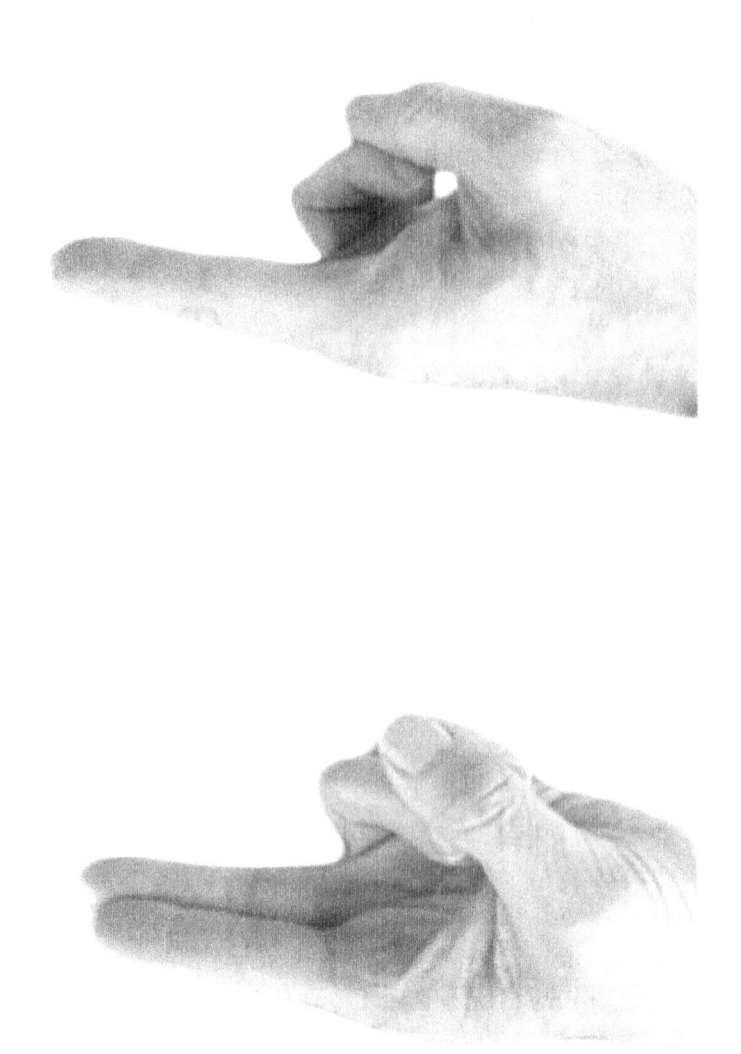

Figure 7: The sword-pointing hand shape

be at least minimally present in both hands all the time (maintaining your sword grip and the pointing fingers shape). This drill automatically enforces Tai Chi's *mind into hands* requirement. Your mind is naturally attracted into your hands and extends into the sword itself.

Probably you'd like an exact formula specifying the position of the pointing fingers hand relative to the sword hand. Don't get too hung up on that kind of physical stuff. Just keep the *idea* that the pointing fingers are energetic backup for the sword hand. The off hand remains a few inches behind it, but nearby. Feel it is energetically reinforcing the cut's power. Experiment a little with the relative position of the hands. Make this drill your own – *steal this drill*.

The YANG cut is with sword gripped palm down and cuts to same side of the body. If, for example you are holding the sword in your right hand, the YANG cut ends with your waist turned to the right, your weight shifted right, and the sword on the right side. When you reach the end of the YANG cut on the sword-hand side, turn the sword over, such that your palm is now facing upward for the next YIN cut across to the opposite side. The blade tip should be making a dignified, controlled little *u-turn* at the flip. Shift your weight to the opposite leg and turn your waist as you power the cut from the lower half of your body. You should play with occasionally shifting the sword-hand from right to left-handed grip and vice-versa without breaking your rhythm or altering the sword's essentially flat, waist-level cutting arc.

Now here's the icing on the cake – as you perform this drill, keep your mind on the *daling* point at all times. This will ensure that the foot-hands pathway is running at full bore throughout your practice time on the drill. That focus keeps the energy running from feet to the given point (*daling*). The final stretch (*daling* to fingers) is covered by the natural attentive gripping/shaping intrinsic to the drill, as discussed above.

The *daling* focus is what blasts this drill out of the common run and into the select pantheon of greatest internal practices of all time. But you must attend carefully to all the Tai Chi principles for full effect.

This drill embodies and develops the traditional Japanese sword principle of *te no uchi* (手の内) or inner wrist power. The great Sagawa Yukiyoshi was almost alone in teaching the *internal* secret of *te no uchi*, as described in the passage below from the book 孤塁の名人 (*Peerless Master*) by 津本陽 (a direct student of Sagawa):

佐川先生は、合気をかけるには「手の内」が大切であると言われていたという 抜刀術で「手の内」といえば、物体を斬る瞬間に体の全力を両方の手のひらに集中し、八十分の一秒のスピードを発揮することであるが、合気の「手の内」は、敵につかまれた瞬間に自分の手首の感覚で、相手の力を測り、どれほどの力でどの方向に攻めているかを知ることだという 手首を通じ、相手の力と動きを迅速に察知するには肩の力を抜き、手に無駄な力をいれてはならないと先生はいうのである つかまれている手首の筋肉だけに力を集中するためには、意識（イメージ）を強く持たねばならないのだという 「合気は意識だ」と、先生はよくいわれたそうである

Sagawa sensei taught that the concept of "te no uchi" (inner wrist power) was essential in the application of AIKI. In the art of drawing the sword, as soon as the sword is deployed the power of the entire body is concentrated in the inner wrists. In only 1/80th of a second, the AIKI sensing power from your inner wrists enables instantaneous gauging of the opponent's intensity, direction, and complete understanding of his attack. According to Sagawa sensei, this kind of immediate sensing is only possible when all excess tension is removed from your shoulders and hands. The AIKI power is then concentrated into the hands by consciousness alone. Sagawa sensei often stated: "AIKI is consciousness".

In that passage, he's talking about the same timing phenomenon taught in the Tai Chi tradition as *starting later but arriving earlier* (後發先至) and *before his power touches me, my mind has already entered his bones* (彼力尚未及我身, 我意已入彼骨裡). As the Tai Chi

Classics state: *if he doesn't move, I don't move; when he makes even the slightest move, I'm way ahead of him* (彼不動己不動彼微動己先動).

In traditional Japanese martial arts, *te no uchi* (手の内) usually refers to the physical grip, i.e. the physical configuration of hand, palm, or fingers in relation to an object such as a sword or archery bow. Teachers and schools squabble over the details, but rarely does anybody see the depth of Sagawa's point above: that *te no uchi* is not physical shaping or any kind of overt technique. It's a point of mind and energy engagement - not a question of hand mechanics or structure. Sagawa's deeper interpretation of *te no uchi* as a sensory focus point corresponds to this book's teaching of the *mind* guiding the energy to the inner wrist energy point *daling*. The *te no uchi* power of AIKI is deeply congruent with the PENG energy and can be understood and developed through this Circle Slice Drill.

The YANG cut begins in (1) with palm down; continues across the body in (2); and finishes in (3) with weight shifted and waist turned, palm still facing down.

Tai Chi PENG

The YIN cut begins in (4) with palm up; continues across the body in (5); and finishes in (6) with weight shifted and waist turned, palm still facing up.

7 Poses: Structural Basics

*The rabbit snare exists because of the rabbit.
Once you've got the rabbit, you can forget the snare.*

- Zhuangzi

I've extracted seven representative poses from the ZMQ37 Tai Chi form to serve as our workhorses. There are many other postures and later you can choose any posture you like for your continued work on the principles - after you've understood them properly. My teacher has pointed out that there are 37 postures in the form, and imagine if you attended a party with 37 other guests, you could always find at least one person you like. So you can find a pose that suits you. Please remember that forms and postures are merely placeholders to keep your mind in the game.

For now, I'm going to use these seven to illustrate key points of the energy development method. Apart from these seven, however, there is a useful basic standing position, called *Preparation Posture*.

Preparation Posture　　預備勢 (yùbèishì)　　*Double*

Unlike every one of the other poses in the form, this one is 50-50 weighting across both feet (indicated by *Double* at the end of the name line above). I mentioned earlier that the most important principle is to always distinguish a strong and a weak leg in every pose, and never have it as a mush of even weighting. But this pose is an exception. We use this posture just to settle ourselves down. We'll have 50% weight on the right and 50% on the left.

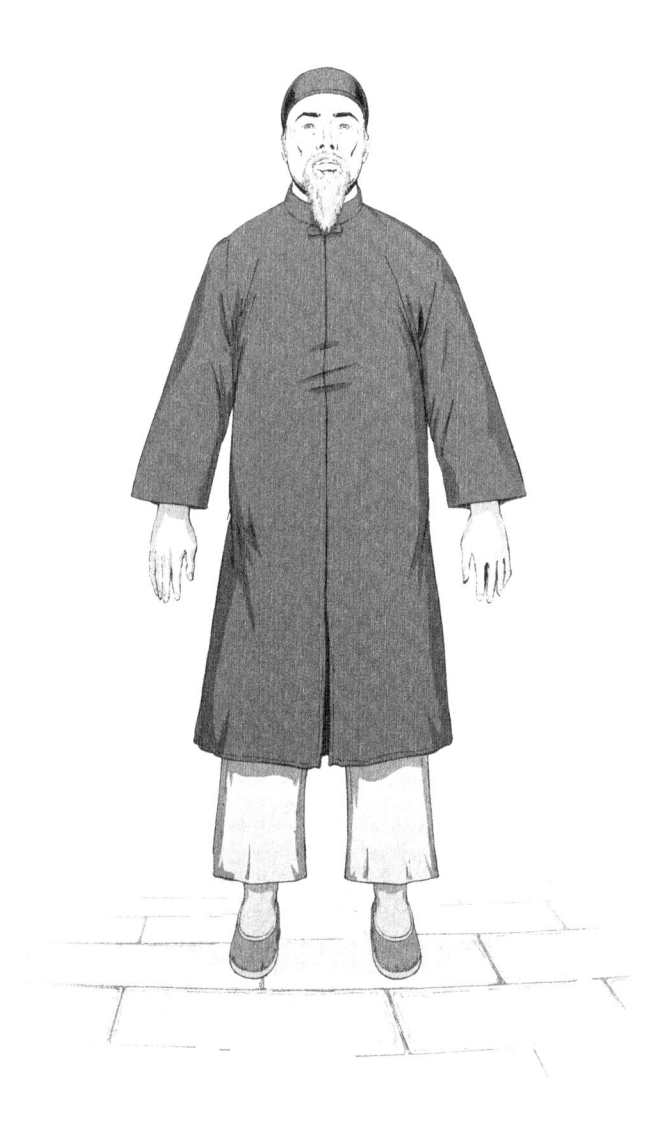

Figure 8: Preparation posture

We stand upright, and form the hands into Fair Lady's Hand. When we first take the position, our hands are held naturally. For most people that means the fingers are slightly curved and the hands hanging at the sides of the body. From there, we can get to Fair Lady's Hand in three steps:

1. Move the arms as a whole, without changing the natural position of the hands and fingers at all, straight out to the front just a little, forming about a 5 degree angle to the body.

2. Then rotate the forearms slightly such that the backs of your hands face directly to the front. Again, treat your hands as dead, just frozen into their original natural position, same as in Step 1.

3. Finally, extend the fingers. Only that, just extend your fingers. You shouldn't need to do anything more because your arms are already in position.

Approaching it this gentle, deliberate way avoids the rushed, harsh mentality of thinking: *Well, time for Tai Chi* and then *bang* jolting your hands into a fixed shape. That's not the spirit of what we're doing here. This 3-step method allows your hands, arms and mind to settle into the right shape, rather then being forced. So begin by feeling the earth under your feet - then in three steps: arms slightly forward, rotate backs of hands to front, extend fingers.

Now we can take a moment to check all the principles from the previous section – relaxation, upright body, sunken shoulders and elbows, natural breath, etc. All our basic principles can be fully manifested through this one posture – except one. We cannot yet *distinguish substantial and insubstantial* because in the Preparation Posture we are still double-weighted.

Golden Rooster on Single Leg

金雞獨立 (jīnjīdúlì)   *Free*

This is the first of the seven training postures. In Rooster pose you have literally only one support leg. This pose is thus perfectly suited to introduce the practicalities of the principle of single-weighting, and for learning to distinguish *substantial* from *insubstantial*. The non-supporting foot is visibly raised off the ground (hence the *Free* designation at the end of the line).

Figure 9: Golden Rooster on Single Leg

Separate Leg

分腳 (fēnjiǎo)   *Free*

This pose is essentially a low kick. It teaches both obvious single-weightedness, and also the idea of extension. You can use this pose to work on the principle introduced earlier of *extend consciousness* – through both arms and the kicking leg. The hands are held in Fair Lady form at a 45 degree cant.

Figure 10: Separate Leg

Repulse Monkey

倒攆猴 (dàoniǎnhóu)   *Zero*

In this pose, the distinction between strong and weak leg will no longer be as visibly obvious as it was in the first two poses above. But that principle is always in force and it's always essential. Here the weak leg is placed on the floor. But don't be fooled – it still bears none of the body weight (indicated by *Zero* on the line above). The feet are shoulder width apart, and parallel, both pointing straight forward (not toes out, as in other Tai Chi styles). One foot in front the other in the rear. The front hand lines up with the front foot. The passive hand is completely relaxed by the side of the rear leg, but don't lose consciousness of Fair Lady's Hand. Fingertips of the forward hand align with your shoulder, not higher or lower, not to the left or right. You should be able to test the 100% back weighting by lifting the front foot a centimeter or so without any effect on your balance or posture.

Even though the basic condition for this pose is the 100 – 0 weighting distinction, it's also a good test case for introduction of one important element of the eventual standing method. That is the distinction between *Zero* and *Resting*. The *Zero* condition is obvious, and has just been described. The *Resting* condition means that the weak leg bears *no more than its own weight*. The leg itself, as a body part, has some weight. When you allow the weak foot to bear the weight of *only the leg itself*, I will call that condition *Resting*. When you attempt this posture, try switching back and forth between the two conditions, Zero and Rest, until you clearly grasp this distinction. You'll feel the leg muscles slightly engaging to achieve the Zero condition, whereas in the Resting condition they can be absolutely relaxed and soft as tofu.

Figure 11: Repulse Monkey

Raise Arms

提手 (tíshǒu)   *Zero*

This pose has exactly the same feature as the Repulse Monkey pose. That is, the weak leg bears no weight at all in the basic form of the posture. The light foot, instead of being flat to the floor as in Repulse Monkey, touches only at the heel, while the front part of the foot is raised a bit from the floor. But be careful not to tense the instep while doing that. It's a very gentle raising gesture. The rear foot is opened at a 45-degree angle. For the arms, the palm of the retracted arm faces the inner elbow of the extended arm. Try to orient your waist straight frontwards, to the extent you can. Here again, the really important thing is the distinction between keeping the front leg at Zero (no weight at all) vs. Resting mode (the leg bears its own weight only). As in Repulse Monkey, play with this distinction until you really feel it.

Figure 12: Raise Arms

Wardoff

掤 (péng)   *Resting*

Now we move to a different class of pose. The first example is Wardoff (the Chinese name is *peng*, a terminology coincidence that has given rise to the misunderstanding about PENG energy that I discussed earlier). This is an example of the front-weighted 70/30 weight distribution, the most common type of pose in the ZMQ37 system, and the most difficult to understand.

Figure 13: Wardoff

Before I get to the subtleties of weight distribution, I'll cover a few basic physical points. First is front knee over toe. This refers to the front leg. The knee is aligned directly over the front toe. Not to exceed it going forward, nor to the rear. Neither to left nor right. Then, the waist is kept strictly facing forward, you can think of it as *navel facing front*. The waist does not angle to the open side as in the front stance of many other styles. The inguinal crease is bent, to keep the front thigh, if not actually quite parallel to the floor, then at least "seeking parallelism". It's like sitting in a folding chair – body upright, legs well bent. The rear foot is flat and the rear knee bends gently in natural conformance with the low height requirement.

The key thing is the relative weighting between front and rear legs. The several back weighted postures above are fundamentally Zero, in that the weak leg bears no weight at all in the most basic style of those poses. However, I also introduced the Resting mode as an alternative practice for those poses. That meant the leg bore only its own weight. This wasn't so terribly hard to understand for the back weighted poses already given. Now we apply the Resting concept to this front-weighted pose, Wardoff, where it seems a bit trickier at first.

This kind of posture almost invites double weighting. It's certainly very difficult to get 100% of our weight onto the front leg without leaning the upper body, but we don't need to get 100% to the front, only 70%. But we need to be really strict about that 70%. It's easy to fool ourselves with this one, and become subtly double-weighted. Practice feeling the strength of your forward leg and the relative ease of the rear leg. Or even try imagining that, due to a cactus spine under your rear foot, you don't dare to put any more weight on it than strictly necessary. I will discuss further technical details relating to the 70/30 weight distribution in the next section.

Single Whip

單鞭 (dānbiān)   *Resting*

Single Whip is an iconic Tai Chi pose. Like Downward Dog in yoga, it's often used as a visual shorthand for the entire art. They say in yoga that *sirsasana* or headstand is the king of *asana* (posture practice) because of its comprehensive benefits. Likewise, for Tai Chi, Single Whip does it all. We again begin with the 70/30 front weighting, everything as for Wardoff above: front knee over toe, rear foot flat, rear knee naturally aligning with rear foot, waist facing front, bend the inguinal crease. The right arm extends directly out from the shoulder. The right hand takes on the distinctive 'beak' shape wherein all four fingers meet the thumb. The left hand keeps Fair Lady hand shape, with extended fingers not higher or lower than the shoulder, nor to left or right. The same weighting principle applies here as in Wardoff: a very definite distinction between the main support work done by the front leg compared to the relative non-involvement of the rear leg, which is as close to the feeling of Rest as you can manage.

Most of the poses in Tai Chi concentrate on a given trajectory or type of gestural energy, such as closing or opening, advancing or retreating, raising or lowering, extending or retracting, etc. Somehow despite its simple appearance, Single Whip gives you the feeling of doing all that at once, in one spherically omni-directional stance. When we integrate the internal work in a later section, this pose will take you farthest. It's a bigger wave to surf than any of the other static postures.

Figure 14: Single Whip

Weaving Lady

玉女穿梭 (yùnǔchuānsuō)   *Resting*

Again, one further example of the 70/30 front weighted type of pose. The lower body from the waist down here is identical to the other two 70/30 poses, but Weaving Lady is included because it gives a good workbench for another principle (which is always operative but made visually obvious here) *Sink shoulders and elbows.* The principle applies just the same even though here the hands are raised above shoulder level. The forearms are canted inward towards each other, creating a triangular shape with a visibility window between the upper and lower hands – don't block your sightline. Keep the shoulders and elbows as sunken and relaxed as possible.

Tai Chi PENG

Figure 15: Weaving Lady

61

Insubstantial and Substantial Leg

Given that the most important principle (after the Relaxation prerequisite) is the distinction between substantial and insubstantial, I'd like to re-emphasize that all seven of our workhorse poses just introduced are essentially *one-legged poses*. All of them, not only the obvious kicks, embody the principle of single weighting, or having one leg doing most of the support work, like a single tree trunk.

If you think that both legs need to be strong, you're going to end up with the mechanical bracing principle that's already been illustrated with the door bar. You'll wind up leaning forward, as though you're trying to push through a solid wall, and also tightening your rear leg for that physical leverage. This 'wall pushing' configuration is double-weighted and will take you far from internal energy training.

The idea that you have only one leg was illustrated in JUICE as below, showing the idea of 'posting' the strong leg by feeling it is pushing into the ground, while merely 'placing' the weak leg (either in Zero mode or Rest mode, as explained above).

There are various philosophical and bio-mechanical explanations of why this idea should result in greater internal energy harvest. I'm not sure anybody really understands it deeply, but the theory doesn't matter much. Here we are interested in the practical performance of the principle. Whenever you can really feel that substantial/insubstantial distinction in the legs, the energy is amplified exponentially.

Tai Chi PENG

Figure 16: The substantial leg is *posted into* the earth, the insubstantial leg is *placed on* the surface

This point has been noticed in all the systems of internal work. Here's a quotation from Xingyiquan Master Guo Yunshen (1829 - 1898) that perfectly sums it all up (from Sun Lutang's book, the chapter titled: 郭云深論形意拳)

後足用力蹬勁, 如同邁大步過水沟之意

(hòu zú yòng lì dēng jìng, rú tóng mài dà bù guò shuǐ gōu zhī yì)

Your rear foot holds strength as though getting set for a big leap across a stream.

Master Guo calls out the "rear" foot. His instruction is offered in the context of Xingyiquan's postures which are mainly rear-weighted, especially their primary static practice of *santishi*. But if I change one character here, his brilliant observation becomes universally valid for Tai Chi also. We just need to substitute the character 獨 (single: dú) in place of 後 (rear: hòu) at the beginning, making it:

獨足用力蹬勁, 如同邁大步過水沟之意

*A **single** foot holds strength as though getting set for a big leap across a stream.*

This now perfectly expresses the primary universal teaching of internal power development. And the seven Tai Chi poses are the perfect workbench.

Now let's talk just a little about the structure of this. If we are performing one of the kicking postures, such as Separate Leg, or the 100/0 rear-weighted poses, it's very easy to understand. You obviously have only one supporting leg. But what's happening with ZMQ37 Tai Chi's 70/30 poses? If the 70/30 split were rear/front we might be in danger of becoming 'door braces'. But it's 70/30 as front/rear. What can be done with this configuration, in terms of our Rest concept?

First of all, the numbers: 70/30. That's the conventional split in most ZMQ37 Tai Chi training. I'd like to push that further and say it's almost 80/20, or if it isn't actually that, you should *feel* as though it's 80/20. If you're thinking 70/30 you'll probably end up a little bit double-weighted.

With 80/20 feeling, the rear leg feels as though it's supporting very little more than its own weight. The best anatomical reference that I've found for this summarizes a lot of work on cadavers and other methods to conclude that a single leg accounts for about 20% of overall body weight (Paolo de Leva, 1996: *Adjustments to Zatsiorsky-Seluyanov's Segment Inertia Parameters.* Journal of Biomechanics 29 (9), pp. 1223-1230). Other references may disagree by three or four percentage points, but that 20% figure suits this Tai Chi method very well.

The simple idea of *Resting* the leg was already introduced for the 100/0 poses. If we accept the 20% leg weight figure, and if while practicing we push the 70/30 toward 80/20, at least in our minds, then even these front-weighted poses become "single legged" in the same way as the *Rest* mode of the rear-weighted poses. You want to feel the rear foot is doing little more than supporting the weight of its own rear leg – even in these "70/30" poses. Of course, the rear leg helps with balance also.

7 Poses: Relaxation Protocol

Now we'll make a second pass over the seven training poses previously introduced, this time with an eye for how to maximally relax. Relaxation is the Prime Pre-Requisite for the energy training. It's not enough to do the postures to physical perfection, as though you were a dancer or choreographer. Dancers, yogis, and other kinetically talented people can easily and perfectly assume any posture. You show them something once and they do it perfectly.

But those people aren't relaxed. I've done partner contact or martial arts drill work with well over ten thousand people of every imaginable training background. Dancers and yogis who can do splits and contortions do not have the esoteric Tai Chi type of relaxation. When people who excel at kinetic mimicry perform a pose, they appear perfect. But when they're touched by somebody who knows Tai Chi, they'll instantly topple, because they aren't relaxed in the sense that we require.

The following illustrations repeat the seven training poses already introduced. But now, for each pose, a teacher demonstrates how to help with total elimination of tension. When a partner supports a part of your body, you can entirely withdraw all tension – even that minimal bit of tension needed to maintain the basically relaxed Tai Chi pose itself (for the given body part). It's easy to work on the arms in this way, and later you can try to replicate the same feeling in your legs and even torso. Alternatively, a training partner can directly apply this Relaxation Protocol to your legs or trunk, using exactly the same principle as with the arms.

In applying the Relaxation Protocol, the training partner begins by merely touching the underside of your arm. You don't need to change at all, at first. Then you gently withdraw tension, little by little, from your arm. This means that in order to maintain the same correct shape of the pose, you are gradually relying more and more on the partner for support. As you withdraw more and more tension, your arm will feel heavier and heavier to the partner - without any alteration to your pose at all. Trust the partner to support your arm entirely. It's amazing how much tension you can still withdraw, even when you think you're done.

A sensitive partner can diagnose it for you, telling you: *No, not yet... let even more go, I've got you* – that kind of thing. Your arm will end up feeling very heavy to the partner. At the maximally relaxed stage, if the partner were to suddenly withdraw support, your arm would plummet "lifelessly" to your side. But the partner should not do that; this is a very gentle, trusting training protocol.

From that maximally relaxed point, you should consciously re-introduce just enough tension to resume the pose on your own. Do that slowly and gradually, in coordination with the partner's supporting less and less of your limb's weight. As the partner withdraws all support, you should then be back in fully independent mode with the pose – but if you've both done it right, your arm will still feel much more relaxed and much heavier than before – even with the same pose shape. Using arbitrary relative figures, we can say that if you began the session with tension 100 in your arm, then with the partner's support you drew it down to 0, then when you reintroduce, you'll feel you only need 50 to maintain the same shape you began with. Then when you practice on your own, you try to reproduce that same feeling of relaxed soft weight that you felt during the exercise.

Posture Support Zones

Golden Rooster: raised leg, raised arm

Separate Leg: raised leg, either arm

Repulse Monkey: unweighted leg, raised arm

Raise Hands: either arm, unweighted leg

Wardoff: raised arm

Single Whip: either arm

Weaving Lady: both arms together, either arm singly

This method is unlimited. For example, in the ZMQ37 form there's one posture wherein you cant the upper body forward (進步栽捶). Basically you're leaning into a low punch. For this pose, the Relaxation Protocol could be taken to its ultimate extreme – a partner could support your entire upper torso with the same withdrawal/reinjection type of interaction, for understanding tension.

Tai Chi PENG

Figure 17: Golden Rooster on One Leg with Relaxation Protocol

Figure 18: Separate Leg with Relaxation Protocol

Figure 19: Repulse Monkey with Relaxation Protocol

Figure 20: Raise Arms with Relaxation Protocol

Figure 21: Single Whip with Relaxation Protocol

Figure 22: Wardoff with Relaxation Protocol

Figure 23: Weaving Lady with Relaxation Protocol

Feeling the Hard Wave

In the night of Brahma, Nature is inert,
and cannot dance till Shiva wills it:
He rises from his rapture and, dancing,
sends through inert matter
pulsing waves of awakening sound.
And lo! Matter also dances.

- Ananda Coomaraswamy

This book deals with what I'm now calling PENG energy. In JUICE, I referred to that as the "soft wave" or SURGE-2. It's a groundswell of power rippling through your body from feet to head and arms. It's a warm, sparkling, hydro-electric kind of feeling. But prior to the soft wave, you will begin to experience its kid brother – the hard wave.

The hard wave is distinctive and while interesting, it does not invoke the same experience of bliss or the drug-like pleasure of the soft wave. But it's fun, and experiencing it is an essential step on the road to getting into the soft wave through which the deeper levels of PENG energy will manifest.

The soft wave is a distinctive motion of the energy. I used water imagery earlier. Water can be either a state (dewdrop, puddle, lake) or a flow (river, ocean current, tide). As a flow, it can be either continuous like a current, or alternating like a sine wave, or AC electricity.

And when water alternates as a wave, there are again two possibilities. It can be like the whitecaps breaking on the shore with a hard, fast, thumping rhythm. Or like the gentle long ocean swells, which are much more powerful but which may never break. The difference between the Surge 1 (hard wave) which I discuss at length in JUICE, and the Surge 2 (soft wave) is very much like the difference between waves breaking on the shore vs. those long ocean swells, which arise from a single pulse of energy traveling miles through the sea.

Even though this book and all long-term serious Tai Chi training is ultimately focused on the soft wave, let's now get a bit more clarity on the hard wave. You will need to go through this phase of experiencing and somewhat understanding the hard wave, on your way to the really good stuff. First thing to note, the hard wave is slightly correlated to the breath. It isn't entirely reducible to breathing, and this doesn't change the fundamental principle introduced earlier: *breathe naturally*. But you will be able to use the breath initially to observe and calibrate the hard wave feeling.

Think of your breath rate as the 'fundamental frequency'. If you've ever done Fourier transforms or harmonic analysis (digital signal processing), you know that there's always a base rate in any periodic signal – the lowest, slowest frequency. As the base, or fundamental, cycles up and down, the higher frequencies and harmonics ride on it. In the same way, the hard wave, which is cycling at a slightly faster rate, rides on the fundamental frequency established by the (slower) breath rate. There are about 3 or 4 internal energy pulses for each breath action (a breath action is either one single inhalation, or one exhalation, so two breath actions together make up one complete breath cycle).

At first, the hard wave is a phenomenon you will *notice*. Not something you *do*, that you make happen. You allow it to happen by being sufficiently relaxed, and weighted properly in the soles of your feet.

This vibration will begin to come through at roughly the rate I specified above. Every physical object – a Coke bottle or anything – has a natural resonance. If it is struck, it will vibrate at its own natural frequency, not at the frequency of some other object. That's what this feels like. It isn't a dog shaking himself, or pugilistic Parkinson's, or *kriya* yogic movements or anything else.

One way to show the hard wave is to hold something loose (in JUICE, I mentioned a long key chain as a possible trial object) and then allow the hard wave to happen. As you drop your breath and energy at least as deep as your *dantian*, or better, to the soles of your feet if you can, the object will begin to swing at the rate of the hard wave. At first you may tend to feel it for the duration of a single breath action (thus, 3 to 4 pulses only), usually an inhale, and then "lose" it on the following exhale. Over time, it will persist across any number of breath actions, finally becoming independent of breath actions altogether.

You stop it by no longer allowing it. It doesn't feel the same as deliberately shaking yourself, then deciding to stop shaking yourself. It's more that the potential for this vibration is always present, but normally suppressed. When you allow it, it comes through until you disallow it.

Key Point: At just the moment the hard waves stops, one full pulse of the soft wave will surge up from your feet through your head, arms, and hands. That's the fun stuff.

At first, it may be necessary for you to generate the hard wave every time, before experiencing one soft wave pulse at the shutoff. Later you will understand the soft wave feeling and learn to generate and control it *independently*. At that point you don't need to fiddle around any more with the hard wave. It's merely a gateway drug to the real thing, the soft wave.

Tai Chi PENG

As I've stated, the hard wave is something you *notice*, not something you *do*. In some people the hard wave may be noticed locally at first. For example, some people may first notice the hard wave only in the abdomen. But soon enough it will be felt as a full body experience. At that point, it's useful to learn to control it to some degree, as an exercise in refining your internal energy perception.

So after you've recognized and experienced it in the process just described, one way to play with it is to learn to localize it. That is, learn to restrict it to one part of the body only. You can experiment with consciously and deliberately localizing it somewhere, and the legs are best for that. You end up experiencing the hard wave vibrations in the legs only, while the upper body remains completely still.

You can begin by allowing the full body hard waves. Then, concentrate your mind on the area from the *dantian* to the soles of your feet. The hard wave will move and restrict itself mainly to that zone. It's another amazing feeling, and it's good training for mental control. You will feel the muscles and bones of your legs, from hip to ankles, quivering and vibrating to the same natural resonance, roughly 3 or 4 Hz, as they were in full-body mode. Your upper body remains unaffected, entirely still. As with the full body waves, you can stop this any time with your mind, and again you will experience the full body 'surge' of the soft wave from the feet when you do so.

So there are several distinct conditions, which we can compare to the motions of an airplane propeller. The first condition, with neither type of wave running, is analogous to a stopped propeller. The hard wave can be compared to the propeller in a lazy "check out" mode, with the plane standing on the tarmac, prop slowly rotating – with the blades still visible. The soft wave is comparable to the propeller at full speed – it speeds up to the point that you can't see it any more.

This state is comparable to the beginning stopped state, in that no motion is visible. The Chinese say 物极必反 (wùjíbìfǎn), meaning 'extremes cycle into to their opposites'. But though the soft vibration state superficially resembles the initial motionless state, in fact it's as different as the high-speed propeller is from stopped one.

It may seem paradoxical, but even though the physical motion of the hard wave ceases when the soft wave surges through, in fact the vibrations have ramped up to a much faster, imperceptible rate which are experienced as a unitary single combined surge – the soft wave. Although it's experienced as a cosmically mystical thing, it can be analogized to basic physics.

A very low frequency tone can be heard as individual pulses of sound. But a higher pitched tone will be heard as a single sustained note because the individual pitch periods have become too short and too close together in time to be perceived separately. These teaching points don't mean that these energies are physical in the normal sense, only that there exist pedagogically useful analogies in the ordinary physical world.

In the Introduction, I mentioned the idea of RIDE – *Recognize, Initiate, Direct*, and *Extend*. I've now covered all components of this concept. But to return for just a moment to the surfing metaphor, I can take the word as a whole, RIDE, and apply that to the experience of training the soft wave. As you do the postures and begin to feel the soft surge by this training process, at first you'll feel only a single surge of the soft wave.

For example, you'll start with the hard wave, let that run for a minute or so, then disallow it, which will shut down the hard wave and instantly trigger the soft wave. The soft wave will surge through you once and that's it. You'll have to start at the beginning to experience it again. This is like paddling out to the break line, then waiting for the right moment to catch something coming up, then paddling into the incipient wave like crazy, then struggling up on your board for a few seconds ride – then you're dumped.

But over time, once you get the first soft surge going, you'll learn to extend that surging, from feet to head and hands, indefinitely. Instead of a *pulse*, it can be experienced as a *continuous* surge (more like a strong river current than a series of waves). This is analogous to the nice long elegant RIDE enjoyed by the expert surfer. So play with it until you get that.

Whether hard or soft, it's difficult to convey in words how the waves feel. The best I can come up with is the earthquake analogy I used in JUICE. Another possibly useful comparison is to actual ocean waves – not as metaphor this time, but as felt experience. Imagine standing at that certain point in breaking surf, just at the point where your feet still barely feel sand beneath you, when you're almost out of your depth. As long as no wave surge comes through, you can stand fairly steadily. When a wave surge comes, you feel totally lifted – every cell in your body - *whoosh* – up all together in a quick heft. In the beginning, the soft wave is an internal version of that feeling. Later it's even more intense.

In the beginning, as with an ocean wave, it isn't something you *do*, it feels like something *done to* you. The ocean wave comparison may be flawed, because it suggests a *unitary* effect, rather than the sequential pulse depicted in the illustrations, but somehow the overall feeling of this is comparable to the soft wave experience.

If you are a particularly sensitive person, you may be able to get a very small sense of it from the first moment or two of an elevator ride, as the pressure wave starts at your feet and quickly spreads through your body. But none of these physical world examples conveys the sheer pleasure and wonder of the Tai Chi PENG wave.

Please understand that this is *not* a wave of kinetic or muscular motion (not even relaxed muscular pulsing). It is an entirely independent phenomenon. Too many practitioners these days believe that if they can shake a little loose physical jolt up through their body, that's the internal pulse. That's completely wrong. That can be learned in 10 minutes – the internal energy waves will require a greater investment of time and thought.

A series of pictures may give some sense of it. Below, the wave is shown originating at the sole of the foot of the strong, or *substantial*, more weighted leg. It then rises up the legs, through the torso, to the head and it ends in the arms and hands. This sequence shows the feel of it about as well as any graphic possibly could. The hard and soft waves both have the same path of propagation – it's only their felt quality that differs. The pictures below show how it feels, not how it looks (the energy is invisible).

After some time refining your ability to initiate and direct the waves (hard or soft), you'll begin to feel what in JUICE I called STATE-2. This is a motionless condition where your body's various elements feel as though transformed into a single smooth, pure substance. It's as though you've jumped from a mechanical body, straight past the vacuum tube phase, straight into solid state.

The waves have been traveling through you, from feet to fingers. But when you reach this *state*, you feel there's no distance between any two points on your body. Everything is adjacent to, or even overlapping, everything else. The origin (*dantian*), transfer station (feet) and terminal (hands) all merge under the high generalship of the *niwan* point. Tail and tooth are no longer separated, as every point becomes one with all.

This *state* will begin to manifest occasionally on its own, just as the waves did. Gradually it will become common in your practice and finally permanent outside of practice. From that point, you won't need to seek teachers and external guidance anymore, because *if you can feel it, you can maximize it*. Such, I will stress a final time, is the tremendous importance of paying attention to *sensations*.

I pretty much guarantee that when you start to seriously feel the real wave coming through (and I don't mean those little buzzes, tingles, flushes, and hot flashes, I mean the overwhelming flow of really *alien* power bursting up through your legs), your first reaction will be: *Oh my God! Why didn't anybody **tell** me about this before??*

Well, I am telling you right now.

Figure 24: The wave begins at or below the sole of the foot

Figure 25: The wave begins to rise up the SUBSTANTIAL leg

Figure 26: The wave broadens out, rising up both legs

Figure 27: The wave reaches full strength as it unifies from the legs

Figure 28: The wave fills the *dantian* area from below

Figure 29: The wave ripples through the mid-body, trunk, and spinal channel

Figure 30: The wave reaches the head and *niwan*, then descends into the arms and hands

Figure 31: The wave charges the arms and foremost hand with the soft PENG power, extending from the *yuanye* armpit points

7 Poses: Zhangzhuang Overview

*Listen, O lord of the meeting rivers,
Things standing shall fall,
but the moving ever shall stay.*

\- Basava

This is where the rubber meets the pavement. The internal Chinese martial arts practice known as *zhanzhuang* (站樁) involves holding energizing postures statically for long periods of time. The translation usually given is 'standing post' ('post' here is meant to invoke the image of a strong pillar or stake driven firmly into the ground). So, it means to stand upright and strong like a wood or stone pillar.

For example, when I trained in a highly combative, old school branch of Chinese Yiquan under a great lineage master in Beijing, I would arrive at the training hall before 7 AM, take up the basic single-weighted pose of that system, and hold it without moving at all for an hour. At precisely 8 AM, I would switch the weighting from my right leg to my left and hold the same pose mirror imaged on the other side for another hour, until 9 AM.

Only *after* that would the day's regular 12-hour training regimen commence (more complex *zhanzhuang* poses, small movement patterns for developing muscle and nerve sensitivity, strike training on the

TAI CHI PENG

heavy bag, long pole training, push hands / sticky hands, and free sparring).

I've experienced traditional *zhanzhuang* training (the aforesaid Yiquan and others, including the original *santishi* posture that I used to hold for hours at a time when drilling Xingyiquan as a teenager in Taiwan). All the various poses used for *zhanzhuang* training, whether the traditional *santishi* or the more recently innovated 20th century forms of Yiquan, are powerful and useful tools, as far as they go.

In this book I will introduce the use of certain Tai Chi postures in a similar way, static holding for internal development. But there will be a twist on the theme, another turn of the screw. As they say in a Hollywood elevator pitch: *It's the same thing, only different!*

JUICE readers will recognize the illustration of the five Tai Chi boys.

The ideal state of relaxation (the bare minimum of muscle engagement and mental activity to maintain the perfect pose, without crossing over the line into excess tension, or slumping back to mental disengagement) is at the top and can be called the Zero Position. To its left are mentally and energetically disengaged states: -20% and -100% (total collapse). To its right are states of excessive physical and mental tension: +20% and +100%.

The ZMQ37 Tai Chi poses, when performed at their Zero Position, can be held for long periods to acquire all the normal benefits of *zhanzhuang* training. They can develop exactly the qualities that *santishi* standing builds in Xingyiquan students. By holding these Tai Chi poses, you will learn to relax and begin to feel the internal energy sinking and then circulating. You can begin with the sample ZMQ37 poses described in earlier sections of this book.

Now I'll introduce a variant of the basic *zhanzhuang* idea. Let's begin by more closely examining two adjoining positions of the graph – the

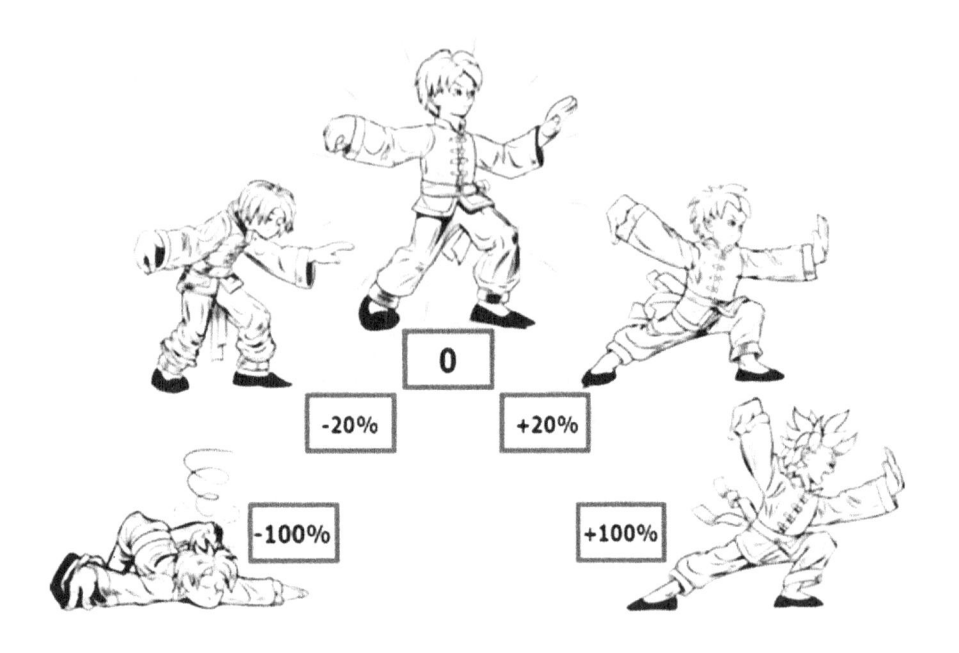

Figure 32: *Five degrees of engagement* - from total collapse (left), through relaxation (center), to extreme tension (right)

Zero Position at the top, and the slight slump to its left, labeled -20% in Figure 33.

The states between the perfect Zero Position and -20% (The Zone) are the 'sweet spot' for practicing active energy standing. The *zhanzhuang* practice is typically static (though the energy may be moving within the body), but the work can be enlivened with a minimal bit of physical movement.

Figure 33: The Zone for *zhangzhuang* 'expanding post' energy work

We begin with the proper Zero Position of any pose, then drawdown or "slump" to -20%; that is, withdraw 20% of our physical and mental engagement from the pose, then "rebuild" or re-engage slowly, starting from the strong foot, back to the Zero Position. Repeat.

That, in essence, is the Drawdown/Buildback method of standing practice. Because it involves re-establishing the full pose from a diminished starting point, I distinguish this from ordinary *zhanzhuang* with a slightly different name: *zhangzhuang* (漲樁). The second character *zhuang* is the same as *zhanzhuang*, but the first character becomes 漲 *zhang*, with the meaning to flow, grow, increase, etc. *Zhanzhuang* is translated as 'standing post', and *zhangzhuang* can be translated 'expanding post'. That's just a terminology thing, but it's useful as a reminder of the difference.

The rebuilding phase is subtle, slow, and gentle. The illustration shows a drawdown of -20%, to illustrate the concept clearly. The slump need not be so outwardly dramatic. It works as well or better to drawdown by -10%, -5%, or even -1%. But those lesser degrees require more sensitivity on your part to distinguish them sharply from the perfect Zero Position. Any degree of drawdown will help you feel the soft wave as you reactivate back to the Zero Position.

In *zhangzhuang*, your movements become very subtle. I call the movements for re-establishing the Zero Position, from any degree of drawdown, *microreactivation*. The eventual goal is to get the full soft wave rush - the state of RIDE - from simply standing in the Zero Position without any *physical* microreactivation. At that point, although the practice returns to the appearance of ordinary *zhanzhuang*, in fact you will have opened up your body to the energy considerably more than before you began.

There are three pieces on the game board of the *zhangzhuang* training: body, mind, and energy. Although eventually they'll be unified, in training you need to be able to distinguish their separate uses and effects.

PHYSICAL: *body structure (pose accuracy) and body endurance, the Zero Position, drawdown/slump, rebuild/microreactivation*

MENTAL: *self-checking your conformance to the pose, controlling the microreactivation process, relaxation, calmness*

ENERGETIC: *the soft wave*

It should be easy to understand the independence of the above three qualities, yet somehow people wrongly conflate them together. For example, it is possible to accomplish the physical and mental aspects of the *zhangzhuang* training (going from Zero Position, to slump,

TAI CHI PENG

back to Zero Position) without experiencing the soft wave at all. That's actually the norm in the beginning.

Conversely, it's possible to experience the soft wave merely by *thinking* it up from your feet, with no drawdown or slump whatsoever. Once you understand it, you can feel it any time, by thinking it up from your feet - whether you are standing in a particular Tai Chi pose or not. Don't make the mistake of assuming that the physical aspect of the microreactivation (straightening up to the fully correct Zero Position) is, itself, the soft wave. It isn't. The microreactivation is merely a physical process you go through to help clear tension and build sensitivity in your body, paving the way for the soft wave to come through *on its own* later.

The key physical aspect of this exercise is that you buildback or microreactivate *from the feet upward*. In particular, you start from whichever foot is *strongest* in the given pose. This conforms to the requirement discussed exhaustively earlier: *separate yin/yang*. You do not physically stand up, or stand higher, as you buildback and microreactivate. You just exert some strength into the ground, through the *substantial* foot – as though you are preparing to leap across a ditch.

That's to get the process going. As you reactivate yourself through the strong leg, your posture begins getting closer to the Zero Position. You kind of "fill out" your legs into a strong yet relaxed stance. Extending your mind into the *yin* leg does that. Don't tense the *yin* leg, just "fill" it with your mind. The energy will follow along on the heels (so to speak) of your extending consciousness.

Then begin to align and straighten up your torso, then shoulders, neck, head, arms and finally fingers, all the way to fingertips. Physically and mentally fill up and fill out your upper body – without any rise in elbows or shoulders. Although we are using a slight physical straightening and extension as training wheels, it's really educating our mind and energy. You are extending consciousness from your grounded *yang* leg into four "limbs" – your *yin* leg, your two arms, and your head.

The leg reactivation is interesting. Most of us can fairly easily relax our arms, when we remember to do so. But legs seem to be different. The poses Golden Rooster and Separate Leg allow us to begin to feel that our *yin* leg is no different from an arm.

At first, as you practice this, you won't feel the real soft wave. I can be almost certain of that. You'll feel the mental and physical process though, and you may be tempted to wonder: *Is this little mental and physical 'unfolding' type of feeling the so-called **soft wave**?*

Answer: *No, it isn't.* Not in the least. If you have decent structure in your ZMQ37 basic poses, you will get the hang of the drawdown and microreactivation pretty quickly. But to experience the real soft wave of PENG energy takes longer.

So don't fool yourself. Prematurely fooling yourself that you've felt it is dangerous because you may conclude that the soft wave is trivial, and seek more interesting pursuits. Conversely, you may feel proud that you've mastered such a recondite activity so easily, and seek greater challenges elsewhere. Both reactions are wrong. Keep playing, and one day you will feel, very subtly, the true soft wave. But even that will be the merest baby dabble. The pleasure and wonder of this PENG wave power are infinite. If you keep at the practice, it will keep on feeding you forever, at ever-greater intensity.

The standing practices of the Chinese martial art of Yiquan at first glance may appear similar in and look and feel to what's just been described. So at this point, the more knowledgeable reader will feel that I am damning Yiquan with faint praise. Doesn't Yiquan, they'd quite rightly point out, have its own "micro movements" in the form of *shili* and *moli* work? Those are Yiquan standing exercises which combine intense mental engagement with barely discernible physical adjustments.

At the 35,000 foot level, the ZMQ37 *zhangzhuang* seems essentially identical to, not even the full scope of Yiquan's *shili*, but to merely a single subtype found in Yiquan's comprehensive catalog of motion vectors. Yes, now it can be told: Yiquan has micro-movements along every possible dynamic axis: opened/closed; front/rear; up/down, and left/right alternations are all trained extensively.

I don't in any way disparage the great internal fighting art of Yiquan. As I have written above, I have trained long and hard in that art, and I have nothing but the highest regard for the system and its outstandingly tough exponents. That said, different people naturally have differing training goals. I am interested solely in the internal energy experience, while Yiquan has many other compensating strengths.

That said, the main differences between Yiquan's *zhanzhuang* 'standing post' / micro-movement method compared with the ZMQ37 *zhangzhuang* 'expanding post' method are:

(1) The Yiquan base poses are not as fully optimized for the greatest possible physical relaxation as are the ZMQ37 poses.

(2) The ZMQ37 method is distinguished by its obsessive attention to the concept of *substantial* and *insubstantial*, and of always beginning the micro-movements from the *one* deeply rooted substantial foot. This yields an extraordinary energy harvest from a relatively easy and short-duration practice regimen.

If you know Yiquan, learn the approach in this book and compare. The internal martial arts connoisseur will discover that, for better or worse, they are as different as whiskey and wine.

7 Poses: The Microreactivation Method

Golden Rooster: Balance can be shaky on these raised-foot poses, so feel free to hold on to the back of a chair in the beginning until you get the hang of it. This is a training option Professor Zheng himself advocated in his book.

Figure 34: Golden Rooster, from slump to the Zero Position. The substantial leg presses strongly through the ground

Separate Leg: Feel that the toes of your kicking leg could actually reach and touch something softly, like fingers. Remember that extension is not tension – they are two different things. You may say: *how can you have extension without tension?* Isn't some tension necessary in this idea of expanding or filling? That may be true at some literal level. But here we care about mind training, so think of an aquarium octopus, with those eight long arms. It appears that they can extend their arms far out into the water without any apparent tension. That's the image we want to hold on to. They curl up - and then they extend.

Figure 35: Separate Leg, from slump to the Zero Position. The substantial leg presses strongly through the ground

An elephant's trunk is also soft as it extends (though seriously powerful when it grabs or whips). (When I trained Shaolin kung-fu as a teen, one of my older classmates was a tough circus/carnival elephant trainer. Whenever he came to the studio for class, he'd park his huge elephant trailer truck in the back alley and the animals would wait out there. He let me wash and feed them sometimes. I know elephants).

In all these *zhangzhuang* microreactivations, the sequence of engagement is: strong leg, light leg, torso, shoulders, arms, hands, and even your head straightens and your eyes brighten and look far outward.

Repulse Monkey: In this pose, balance is no longer a factor, so you can stand in it longer and work with it more deeply. But even in this pose, you still only have one leg; one *yang* or strong leg is doing all the support work. As you microreactivate, feel the mental extension into the *yin* leg. As you do so, it may feel it's floating up off the floor, very slightly. Feel that you are extending consciousness into that leg, just as you are into your arms and head. With this posture we have an additional option that isn't available to us when the leg is actually off the floor, as in the first two poses above. That is, as I mentioned when the pose was first introduced earlier, you can work this pose with Zero weighting of the *yin* leg, or you can rest the *yin* leg on the floor, such that it bears only its own weight. Play back and forth between these two options.

TAI CHI PENG

Figure 36: Repulse Monkey from slump to the Zero Position. The substantial leg presses strongly through the ground

But remember, even when you work on the Rest option, your torso, arms and head will still be microreactivating as before. When in Rest, the leg muscles can be 100% relaxed, whereas in Zero mode you need a slight engagement of the *yin* leg's muscles to keep its weight from being supported by the floor. You must be able to clearly distinguish and understand both modes, but it's in the Rest mode (with otherwise full extension/engagement) that you will most strongly feel the soft wave.

Raise Arms: This is similar to Repulse Monkey, except the foot configuration differs in that the foot rests on the heel with toes gently raised off the floor.

Figure 37: Raise Arms from slump to the Zero Position. The substantial leg presses strongly through the ground

Wardoff: This is the first of the front-weighted poses, so-called 70/30 weight distribution. As I've said, it's better to think of it as 80/20, where the 20% is only the rear leg's own weight and little more. The front leg does almost all the work of supporting your body. It's just the same as the Rest mode of the poses that are more obviously single-support, such as Repulse Monkey and Raise Arms. It's easy to slip into the dreaded double-weight condition. That will happen if, as you microreactivate, you end up coming through both legs instead of beginning very clearly with the *yang* leg. You do want a feeling of extension into the *yin* leg, but that extension is mental, not physical. Remember not to stand up, don't raise the overall level of your pose. Just *fill* yourself.

Figure 38: Wardoff from slump to the Zero Position. The substantial leg presses strongly through the ground

If anything, as you stand, rather than pressing the rear leg into more physical work, try to relax it even more than when you started. One thing that will help you relax your entire leg is to take care that initially your instep, the inner top of the ankle, is totally soft. If you can relax that, probably your entire rear leg is fairly relaxed. If the inner instep is tense then you are probably supporting yourself partially with the rear leg, and in danger of double weighting.

Single Whip: This pose brings in the same overall considerations as Wardoff, above. Of any pose in the entire ZMQ37 set, Single Whip is the one that most embodies everything we need. So if you only have time to work on one pose, it should be this one because you will feel the soft wave more strongly in this pose than in any other of the 7 static poses I've introduced. Then you can try to recapture that feeling in the other poses.

Figure 39: Single Whip from slump to the Zero Position. The substantial leg presses strongly through the ground

Weaving Lady: This is another 70/30 front-weighted pose, like Single Whip. This is the only pose in which the hands are above the shoulders. Therefore be careful not to raise up your shoulders and elbows, keep them sunken and relaxed just as before, in accordance with the basic Tai Chi principle.

Figure 40: Weaving Lady from slump to the Zero Position. The substantial leg presses strongly through the ground

The Final Principle: Waist Activation & Cloud Hands

I presented the Tai Chi Training Principles in a previous section. Every pose we've been working with so far, such as Single Whip and so on, embodies every one of the Principles. Every one of them requires an upright relaxed body, sinking shoulders and elbows, flat lower back, natural breathing, Fair Lady's Hand, distinguishing full/empty, and extension of consciousness.

But there is a remaining Tai Chi Principle, universally cited as one of the Top Ten, that can't be worked in the poses I've covered so far. That's because I've only introduced static postures. We need one more drill to cover the final principle: *Waist Consciousness*.

Waist Consciousness has been labeled in different ways by different experts:

主牽於腰	*Waist leads*	Tai Chi Classics
鬆腰	*Relax the waist*	Yang Chengfu
轉動在腰	*Turn the waist*	Benjamin Lo

Somehow we need to bring the waist into play and for full effect it must involve movement. There's a sequence in any Tai Chi form called Cloud Hands. It's basically revolving the waist and some accompanying gentle arm movements. When this is done in the full ZMQ37 Tai Chi set you move across the floor sideways, to your left with each shoulder-width step. But here we'll clip it down to a stationary exercise with the same or greater energy harvest.

You begin with Preparation Posture. Then turn your waist to your right while raising your right arm to shoulder height, with Beautiful Lady's Hand. Your left arm circles under your right, with the left palm facing upwards toward the right palm above it, as though you are holding a beach ball on your right side. The palms face each other, right above left below. Your gaze is to the right side or at least the right front corner of the room.

Then you repeat the following sequence, first on the right side, then on the left, back and forth alternating, with your weight shifting from side to side as your waist turns. The word 'engaged' is used below to refer to the quality of intense yet relaxed *alertness to sensation* which precedes the action of energy.

Step 1: Drop the upper arm on the outside, while rotating the palms so that they now both face inward to the body. The upper palm is chest level and the lower palm is navel level.

Step 2: Holding your arms relaxed but immobile, let your waist carry you across as you shift weight to the opposite leg

Step 3: Raise the foot slightly while engaging everything (Zero condition)

Step 4: Place the (now empty) foot down, flat, while remaining engaged in all other parts. (Rest condition)

The overall spirit of the method is micro movement. You could turn your waist severely to each side, but you don't need to do it that intensely. Just a light turn to the side, a few inches of turn, is enough. Try to distinguish between *turn the waist* vs. *twist the waist*. Turning is relaxed, twisting is tense.

When you really have the energy running, every time you turn you'll feel the energy sloshing powerfully in your trunk, as though your whole torso were a barrel of thick crude oil. That won't be your physical gut sloshing, that will be your energy gut. This version of the traditional Cloud Hands drill is simple and physically undemanding. It takes little time and minimal space and yields a strong energy harvest.

This version of Cloud Hands can be thought of as a kind of *micro shiko*. *Shiko* is the most basic exercise of sumo, which you may have seen on TV if you've ever been to Japan during the sumo season. The sumo wrestlers do a very strenuous exercise, where they alternately put their weight onto a single leg, raising the other as high as possible. They'll raise one leg, then sit down into a very deep squat, then raise the other leg.

This is a great conditioning exercise. And it dramatically embodies our single-weighting principle. But it's physically very demanding. Physical fitness is a great thing, but it's not the subject of this book. The degree of sweat and exertion required to perform *shiko* as the real sumo wrestlers do will overwhelm your initially very subtle stirring of energy. You won't catch the feeling, and you'll end up overlooking the clues that would have led you toward the PENG energy goal.

You could perform the full version of true professional *shiko* many times a day and never feel the PENG power. Sagawa Yukiyoshi, the great master of the internal Japanese martial art Daito Ryu, who was perhaps the greatest master of internal combatives in Japanese history, instructed his closest students to perform one thousand repetitions of *shiko* every day, hinting that they would thereby develop the internal power. One of his most ardent followers reports in his book that indeed, after performing one thousand reps every day for a long period, he began to feel the internal power. But you can imagine how challenging that must have been.

Tai Chi PENG

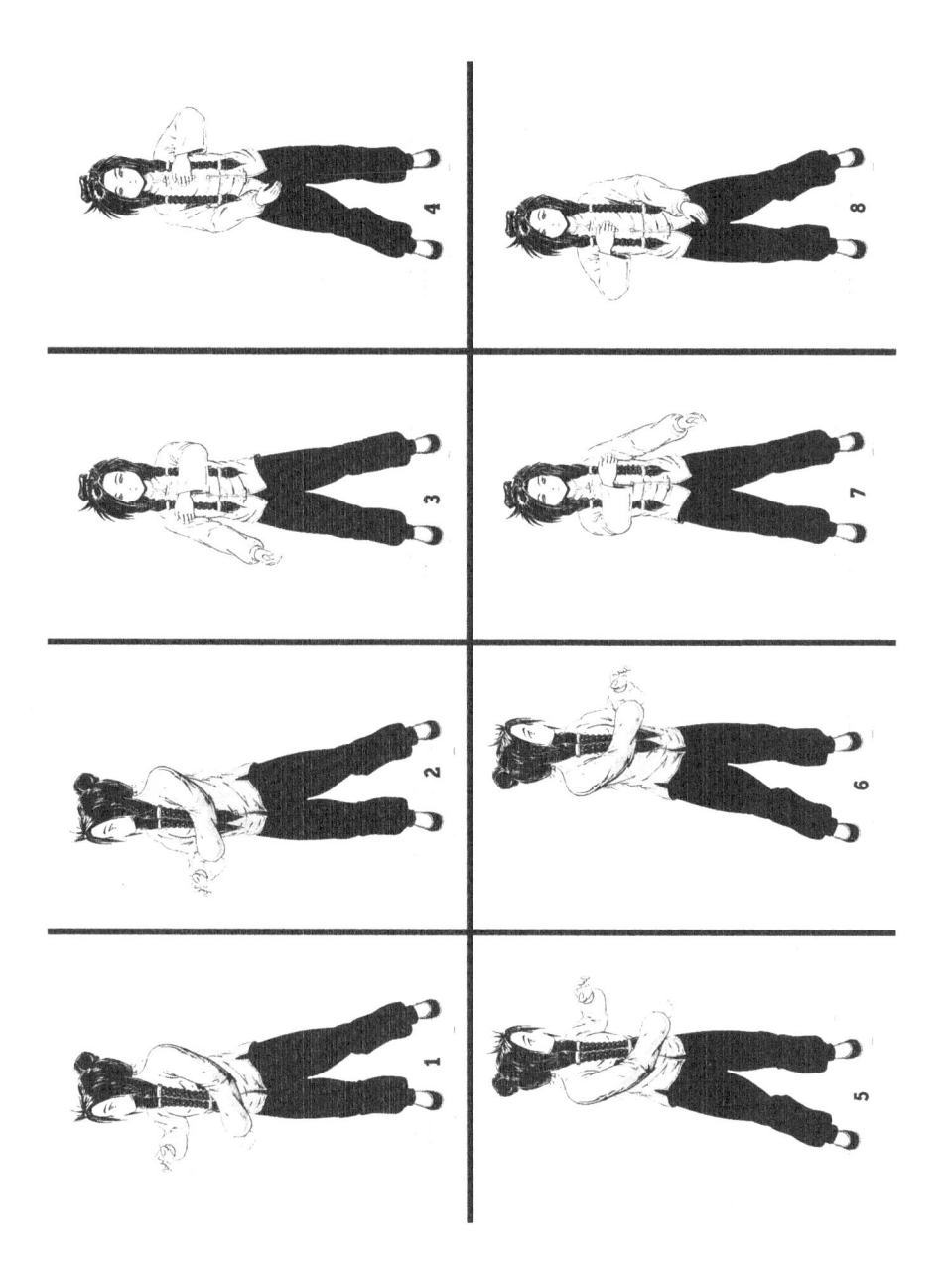

Another student of Sagawa's later pointed out, in a magazine article, that Sagawa himself did not perform the full, extreme professional

Figure 41: A sumo champion wrestler performing the *shiko* exercise

sumo version of *shiko*. Apparently the master elevated his foot much less and stepped down more gently, and reduced or eliminated the squat phase. In other words, it seems that his version of *shiko* was much closer to this Tai Chi version of Cloud Hands than it was to the professional sumo *shiko*.

WHY?

*The same thing I would want from you today
I would want again tomorrow*

- Bob Dylan

The most interesting question remains: *What is the difference, if any, between Tai Chi and Qi Gong?* I'm often asked this, and it has particular resonance for me because I seem to have painted myself into a corner. It's a softball question to most other Tai Chi teachers, because they can cite the normal laundry list of unique mental and physical Tai Chi benefits. But I can't do that. By setting aside almost every feature that normally attracts people to Tai Chi, I've brought this question onto myself.

I've emphasized that, to me, Tai Chi is neither dance, nor cultural appreciation, nor practical combatives, nor physical fitness, nor physical therapy, nor the endlessly touted "improving balance for seniors" or any of the normal clichés of this art. I've been *energy centric* all the way.

However... there's already a vast panoply of traditional and modern Chinese systems that deal precisely with internal energy cultivation, under the umbrella term Qi Gong. Those systems, just like Tai Chi, also talk about circulation and strengthening of the *qi* power and use body points that are borrowed from ancient medical theory such as the

Lower, Middle, and Upper *dantian* and others. These appear to be the same as my approach to Tai Chi. We needn't even restrict the discussion to Chinese systems. The internal energy is now widely known and practiced by Western energy healers, astral projectors, spiritual meditators and others.

Average people now learn to run energy from their hands in a single weekend seminar from teachers of Quantum Touch, Pranic Healing, Reiki, medical Qi Gong, and Matrix Energetics, to name just a tiny sample of the thousands of available programs. A mouse-click brings a torrent of books and videos offering the once-secret teachings of energy masters like Mantak Chia, Robert Peng, and others straight to your living room screen or tablet. Prominent astral projectors can teach you in an hour to form energy balls with your hands and move the energy around your body.

I do not disparage these teachings in any way. After all, we really *are* made of energy, and it shouldn't be strange if, with a bit of motivation and guidance, people can easily learn to feel it. A typical attendee at any of the above seminars can learn in a few hours to do something like what this typical energy healer reports:

> *Ninety percent of my patients feel the energy flow strongly during their treatment. They may have sensations of heat, tingling, of both. Occasionally a patient feels intense cold, even to the point of shaking. When this happens, turning up the heat in the room makes no difference in the experience of cold because it is the healing energy at work. A few patients say they feel as if they are about to rise off the table and float in the air.*

(Presence of Angels: A Healer's Life; J. C. Hugh MacKimmie, 2005, Knowing Heart Publishing)

Given that state of affairs (which is, after all, human progress), where is the place and what is the need for an energy-centric *Tai Chi*? I could get on my high horse here and try to buffalo you with talk about different types of energy, *qi* vs. *jing* and so on. But I want to give a straighter and more personal answer: It's **art for art's sake**. *Ars gratia artis.*

It's my aesthetic preference. By that I don't mean an artistic appreciation of Tai Chi dynamics as dance or theater, the physical performance so many people love. I find Tai Chi quite boring to watch. I'm talking about a deeper aesthetic here, a way of *being-with-energy* that attracts me.

In Chinese there's a phrase: 武比 (wǔbǐ), meaning literally something like trial by arms, which can be applied to any combative contest, like a boxing match or cage fight, etc. See who's the tougher, more kickass man. Who will walk out under his own power? Who champ who chump? That kind of feeling.

Tai Chi, like any activity with ancient martial roots, is sometimes promoted combatively with this *wubi* flavor. After all, 19th century supermeister Yang Luchan was nicknamed Yang Wudi (Invincible Yang) precisely due to his peerless fighting ability, displayed in beating down all challengers. But just as I don't emphasize the purported health benefits of Tai Chi (though I privately know I've hugely harvested them), I don't push it as a fight or self-defense art either. No point in that, because, as noted since ancient times: *the fortunes of war are various.* Real fighting, whether street or sport, has too many variables for me to go around acting like Tai Chi has made me into some kind of fight king. Anybody can "beat" anybody in a given situation. The next guy up would just kick my ass.

Look at people far beyond an average hobby martial artist like me, professionals like Mike Tyson or Manny Pacquiao. Who would have predicted a non-entity like Buster Douglas could take out Iron Mike in his prime? Who'd have thought even a great counterpuncher like Juan Manuel Márquez could send the Pacman to the canvas for almost five minutes with a single perfect punch? When it comes to *wubi*, street or sport, personal skill (including any dinky internal power) does not fully determine the outcome.

And the wisdom that *the fortunes of war are various* even applies to something much less real than boxing, yea, even unto to a mere drill like Tai Chi push hands. Neither I nor any other Tai Chi teacher can guarantee that we'll always be fully charged and ready to zap the next comer. Any given partner may give us trouble or push us on our butt. I have to laugh at those who overtly or covertly try to market push hands as some kind of fight thing. That's really a contradiction.

You've heard of kicking range, striking range, grappling range? Tai Chi push hands is *sucker punch range*. You're in sucker punch range with somebody, yet supposedly training for self-defense therefore you're all up in your fight stance and combat mindset? *It's a contradiction*. Why would you ever be in sucker punch range yet all keyed up for a fight? You should have either never gotten into that range in the first place, or else ended it immediately with a head butt, instep stomp, elbow to the face, or something else realistically effective.

I sometimes joke that people who try to sell push hands as combative training are like the economist who washed up on a desert island. He found canned food but no can opener. The economist had the perfect solution though: *First, assume I have a can opener!* In treating push hands as a fight thing, as a kind of *wubi*, those people are assuming away the biggest problem that martial arts needs to solve: *closing the gap without getting smacked*. *Wubi* is an endless, pointless sucker's game.

But there's another, related Chinese phrase: 文比 (wénbǐ). This *wen* is the word for fine arts, literature, high class activities like that. It's the gentleman's way of comparing power and attainment, where nobody gets hurt or even embarrassed. It's a hidden comparison between the two players - classy, subtle, understated. The aforesaid Yang Luchan and his family were also masters of this refined style.

> *The House of Prince Duan, one of the royal families in the capital, employed a large number of boxing masters and wrestlers —some of whom were anxious to have a trial of strength with Yang Luchan. Yang typically declined their challenges. One day, a famous boxing master of high prestige insisted on competing with Yang to see who was the stronger. The boxer suggested that they sit on two chairs and pit their right fists against each other. Yang Luchan had no choice but to agree. Shortly after the contest began, Duan's boxing master started to sweat all over and his chair creaked as if it were going to fall apart; Yang however looked as composed and serene as ever. Finally rising, Yang gently commented to the onlookers: "The Master's skill is indeed superb, only his chair is not as firmly made as mine." The other master was so moved by Yang's modesty that he never failed to praise his exemplary conduct and unmatched martial skill.*
>
> (Gu Liuxin, The Evolution of the Yang School of Taijiquan)

Now that's what I call *wenbi*! Chinese culture offers even subtler opportunities for this kind of play. For example, when offering a toast and clinking cups, two masters can easily diagnose who is internally stronger from the one quick bump. Likewise, imagine that one diner chopsticks the last succulent shrimp on the platter and attempts to foist it onto the guest of honor. As the honored one politely deflects the proffered crustacean, all becomes known in an instant. Or the

Chinese tradition of a guest preventing his host from troubling to accompany him all the way to the door or down to the gate – a light restraining hug and the phrase: 請留步! (qǐng liú bù)- yet another culturally sanctioned, diagnostic *wenbi* moment.

That kind of stuff, while fun, may seem like childish gaming, and I agree it's mostly just a high-end pissing contest. But it gets to my final, roundabout answer on the appeal of Tai Chi to me. My Tai Chi teacher has that kind of understated yet omnipresent *wenbi* type of Tai Chi power. He has some version of what has described about the Yang ancestors of the classical age of Tai Chi. My teacher hasn't displayed that publically, on the street or in the cage, but I have felt it many times. I don't think it's really much use for anything in the real world, or the modern world. But that's ok with me. I like it. Just as a wine taster prefers certain vintages, we shouldn't need to over-justify mere aesthetic preferences.

I've met, how many dozens or even hundreds of Qi Gong and Nei Gong masters? Yet to my parochial hands and eyes, none of them had my teacher's amazing Tai Chi internal solidity – a power that, in Chen Weiming's great phrase, is *both soft and hard at the same time.*

How to be both a rhino and a snake, all at once? How to stand like oak and bamboo, both in the one body? How to be a tornado and a zephyr? A tsunami and a sprinkle of morning dew? That kind of inner experience is, to me, the essence of Tai Chi. These are the milestones along the infinite pathway of PENG power. That's what I appreciate and seek. Never have I experienced it in any other context. So I continue to pursue Tai Chi forever - *Ars gratia artis.*

The Graphic Tai Chi Classic

The historical origin of the The Graphic Tai Chi Classic *is disputed by scholars. Some swear by the traditional account below, while critics scoff that this is merely a witch's brew of legend, speculation, half-truths, and even outright fabrication. The facts are lost in the dustbin of history. Here, for what it's worth, is the most widely accepted theory:*

Down through the Chinese dynastic millennia, only the elite few, the high Mandarin literati, could read and write. Thus, only officials and scholars knew the essays and epigrams that define the Art of Tai Chi. And even those treasures of world cultural heritage were barely saved by the merest whisker from loss or destruction in the sustained hurricane of cultural cataclysm, battles, warlords, famine, epidemics, invasion and revolution that battered China down the long dark decades of the 20th century.

For example, the only known source text of the primary statement of Tai Chi's methods and goals, Wang Zongyue's collection of epigrams, was found and preserved by lucky chance. A martial arts master happened to hear that an interesting essay had been carelessly tossed into the back bins of a neighborhood shop. That teacher retrieved it, saving it for the ages, and left us only this laconic comment as to its provenance:

聞鹽店有王宗岳拳譜求索得之

I heard that Wang Zongyue's Tai Chi essay was stashed in a salt shop. I went there looking for it, and I got hold of it.

(This document has therefore been nicknamed *The Salt Shop Manual*).

But even now, when Wang's monumental achievement is celebrated around the world in the noonday sun, stories that hint of *another* priceless Tai Chi teaching relic are only whispered in the moonless dark. For it has long been speculated that the Tai Chi Greats of old, fearing that the crumbling of the last dynasty would spell the end of the rarified Chinese literary legacy, decided to take secret countermeasures.

They envisioned a distant future time when the people of the world would finally grow the frick *up*, acknowledge the brotherhood of man, and restore the Art to its rightful place as a practice of peace, fun, and highest self-cultivation. But by then, they fretted, would the cryptic beauty of literary Chinese be no more readable than Egyptian hieroglyphics? Thus, they decided to have the Art coded *pictorially*. And it came to pass that these greatest Masters commissioned *The Graphic Tai Chi Classic* as a secret work, initially kept strictly to themselves, held in trust for future generations.

The *bad* news is that only a miniscule fragment of this monumental artistic achievement has ever come to light. In 1915, as dueling warlords bombarded a certain city and the ancient town walls were blasted to dust, one brave soul dashed into a burning building, re-emerging more dead than alive – but with a certain precious scroll stuffed under his scholar's gown. His only recorded comment was this:

聞辣椒店有漫畫拳譜求索得之

I heard that the Graphic Tai Chi Classic was stashed in a hot pepper shop. I went there looking for it, and I got hold of it.

(This historical treasure is therefore cited by scholars as *The Pepper Shop Manual*).

Tai Chi PENG

The scroll was so badly fire-scorched and bullet-riddled that only a few sections remained legible. But the *good* news is that the few surviving panels of this great transmission – a work so secret that no single glimpse of it has ever been publicly reported – have now been painstakingly restored by world-class art experts, and are reprinted on the following pages for your edification.

邁步如貓行

一羽不能加

蠅蟲不能落

活似車輪

人不知我
我獨知人

Tai Chi PENG

Panel Index

CAT

邁步如貓行 (màibùrúmāoxíng)

Step like a cat.

FEATHER

一羽不能加 (yīyǔbùnéngjiā)

A single feather would oppress you with its weight.

FLY

蠅蟲不能落 (yíngchóngbùnéngluò)

A fly could not alight without setting you in motion.

WHEEL

活似車輪 (huósìchēlún)

Mobilize yourself like a wheel.

X-RAY

人不知我 我獨知人 (rénbùzhīwǒ wǒdúzhīrén)

My opponent does not know me, I alone know him.

Epilogue

> 好花不常開, 好景不常在
>
> - Chinese proverb

> *They say that a good thing never lasts*
> *And that it has to fall*
>
> - Madonna

> *Though the dawn may be coming soon*
> *There still may be some time*
>
> - Gary Wright (Dreamweaver)

The body is already obsolete. Most people working in the human potential disciplines haven't grokked it yet, but we're well on our way to becoming the transient hybrid species that bridges the human race over to its entirely mechanized or virtual/holographic successor.

I don't mean to say that like it's a bad thing. That's probably the best outcome we have any right to hope for, given how we played with nuclear hellfire like toddlers chewing gasoline-soaked rags. And in terms of human suffering, the Rise of the Machines is probably better than descent into a new, cannibalistic Dark Ages type of scene. But it means that the various old-school personal power disciplines, like Tai Chi, which are based on the assumption of a discrete human body, and an un-enhanced, un-networked neural identity, will find themselves increasingly marginalized.

So, people (while I can still call you that) - *carpe diem*! Make hay while the sun shines! Have fun while you can with what you've got on your hands: an Original Model, Anthropoid-Series HUMAN BODY®. You're set up with an all-organic, unalloyed, *homo sapiens neurosomatic bio-complex*, straight off the Darwinian factory floor, which, when operated according to the instructions in this manual, will provide you with many years of Wave and State pleasure.

Acknowledgements

These are some of the Tai Chi people (teachers, classmates, senior role models, partners, friends, students, and fellow travelers) who've made a dramatic difference in my development. Hundreds of others have helped me immeasurably, but these are the core Tai Chi people alone. If I list everybody who's done so much for me, I'll end up with a blubbering 500-page personal memoir instead of this lean and mean floor-shop manual.

Inclusion on this list does not remotely imply endorsement of, or responsibility for, this book. But even though they run screaming to sign 12-month black-belt contracts at the nearest strip-mall Tae Kwan Do academy every time they hear me say it, here's *another huge thank you* to the Tai Chi heart-masters below who helped wake me up inside:

Benjamin Lo, Wayne Abramson, Bert Brown, Tom Campbell, Ed Chan, Pak Chan, Garrett Chinn, Patricia Corrigan Culotti, Robert Davis, Tana Farnsworth, Marvin Feldman, Don Gillaspie, Michael Hackshaw, Anthony Ho, Chien-Liang Huang, Michael Jang, Alan Kempner, Peter Kwok, Terry Li, Daniel Lo, Steve Messenheimer, Kayo Robertson, Al Sambuco, Lee Scheele, Robert W. Smith, Lenzie Williams, Carol Yamasaki, Henry Yu.

Resources

All you need to go forward in your Taiji research is here:

1. The Essence of T'ai Chi Ch'uan - The Literary Tradition
Martin Inn, Robert Amacker, Susan Foe Benjamin Pang Jeng Lo (Translator), Calligraphy by Benjamin Pang Jeng Lo (Illustrator)
IRI Press (2008)

2. Cheng Tzu's Thirteen Treatises on T'ai Chi Ch'uan
Cheng Man Ch'Ing (Author), Benjamin Pang Jeng Lo (Translator), Martin Inn (Translator)
Blue Snake Books (1993)

3. T'ai Chi Ch'uan Ta Wen: Questions and Answers on T'ai Chi Ch'uan
Chen Wei-Ming (Author), Benjamin Pang Jeng Lo (Translator), Robert W. Smith (Translator)
Blue Snake Books (1993)

4. The Lectures with Benjamin Pang Jeng Lo - 4 DVD Set [DVDROM]
Benjamin Pang Jeng Lo
IRI Press; 1st edition (2010)

珊

CPSIA information can be obtained at www.ICGtesting.com
Printed in the USA
LVOW04s2014250814

400820LV00023B/1603/P